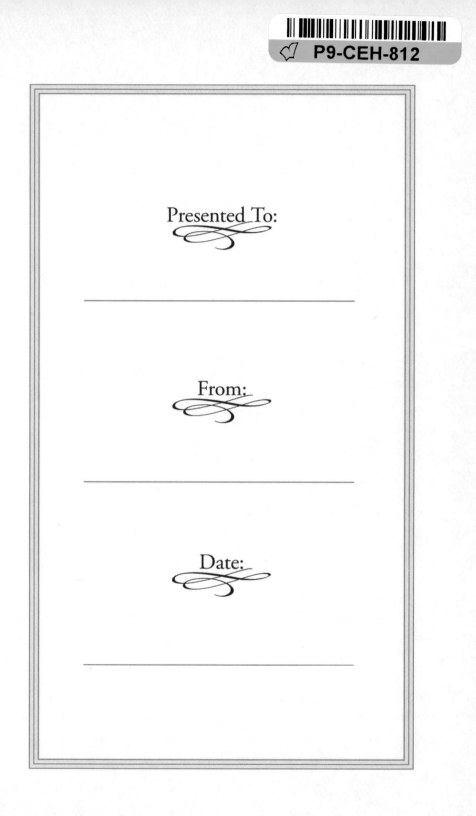

Presented To:

_____

From:

_____

Date:

_____

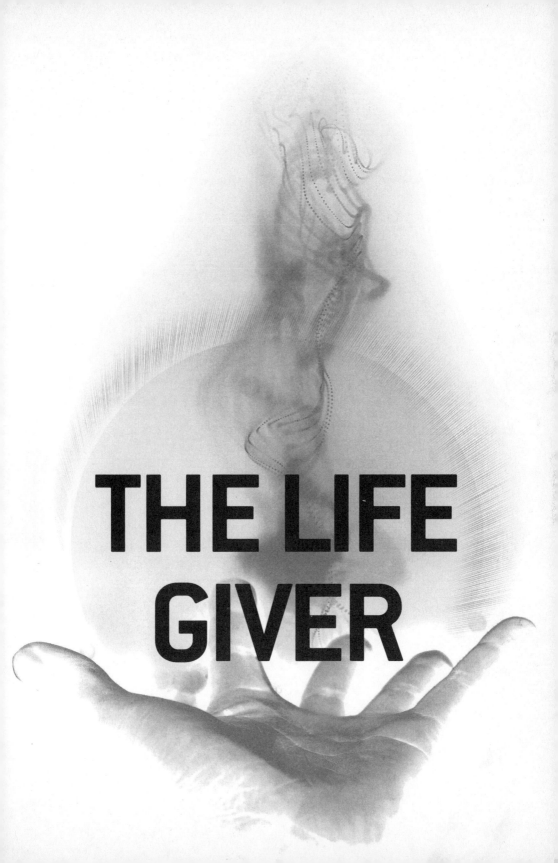

THE LIFE GIVER

ANOTHER DESTINY IMAGE BOOK BY JOEY LETOURNEAU

Revolutionary Freedom

Joey LeTourneau

"...But I Come That You Might Have
Life and Have It in Abundance"
(John 10:10)

THE LIFE
GIVER

DESTINY IMAGE₀ PUBLISHERS, INC.

P.O. Box 310, Shippensburg, PA 17257-0310

"Promoting Inspired Lives."

This book and all other Destiny Image, Revival Press, MercyPlace, Fresh Bread, Destiny Image Fiction, and Treasure House books are available at Christian bookstores and distributors worldwide.

For a U.S. bookstore nearest you, call **1-800-722-6774.**

For more information on foreign distributors, call **717-532-3040.**

Reach us on the Internet: **www.destinyimage.com.**

ISBN 13 TP: 978-0-7684-4142-0

ISBN 13 Ebook: 978-0-7684-8819-7

For Worldwide Distribution, Printed in the U.S.A.

1 2 3 4 5 6 7 / 14 13 12

DEDICATION

To my life-giving family…

Father, I love You! Thank You for *who* You are and for loving me so much! I want to love You more. Here's to the life that Your love gives!

Destiny, my bride, you bring life into every part of mine! You simply shine. Even your laugh gushes life, and I love you with all my heart!

My special daughters, Anna, Ayni, Mercy, and Gali, you bring more life to your mom and me than you could ever know. We bless you to live the Father's life and to live it more abundantly!

To Mom, you have given me life for over 30 years in *so many* different ways! "Thank you" doesn't even begin to express how much you mean to me or the life God is multiplying.

To Dad, who is living and loving large in his heavenly home, thank you! Your life meant so much to mine that even since you left this earth I have continued to inherit life from you in the biggest of ways.

Jackie, thank you for *all* you mean to my life and family. I love you lots, appreciate you, and bless you to live the fullest and most fruitful life God could possibly have for you!

To all my family, your life-giving ways have always modeled what it means to love and embrace everyone, unconditionally, as family. Thank you each very much!

To our Ethiopian family, you mean so much to us. We love you like family, which is how you have always loved us. Thank you! A big part of our heart will always reside in Ethiopia.

To our spiritual family all over, thank you for always offering so much love, life, and support to us in so many different ways. Thank you for partnering with us to give life!

ENDORSEMENTS

We live in such an encouraging time in history when believers all around the world are beginning to realize they were designed to bring hope, life, and restoration. The Body of Christ is recognizing the mandate of the hour and that is to bring the Kingdom to earth. *The Life Giver* is a book written for the purpose to see *you* bring life everywhere you go.

Eric Johnson
Author of *Momentum: What God Starts Never Ends*
Senior Leader of Bethel Church, Redding, CA

I am so excited about *The Life Giver* by Joey LeTourneau. You will not want to put it down as Joey reveals some really great insight into finding your true identity. It's for those who want to get all they can out of life and more!

Doug Addison
Author of *Personal Development God's Way*
www.dougaddison.com

"...I have come that they may have life, and that they may have it more abundantly." —John 10:10

TABLE OF CONTENTS

INTRODUCTION

The thief does not come except to steal, and to kill, and
to destroy. I have come that they may have life, and that
they may have it more abundantly (John 10:10).

WE serve and follow a creative, life-giving God, and He has created us to be creative, life-giving people. He gives physical and spiritual life in an abundance of ways, and He has called us to tap into that life, receive it in abundance, and freely give it out to a world that is waiting, longing, and in need. We must remember that our Father has not only given us life to live, but He has given us life more abundantly to transform. This has left a cry in my heart—and I hope in yours, too. I want more! I want more of Him and the revived life He brings in me. I want more for my family, for my community, for our nation, and I want more of my Father and His life for the world. Life is created to multiply. Our Father gave this life more abundantly, but He has called on us to move forward and pass it on.

I love the above verse, John 10:10, where Jesus reminds us why He came: to give life and to give it *more* abundantly! He is once again reaffirming the mission He announced for Himself from Isaiah 61:1-3, when He began His ministry here on earth (see Luke 4:16-21). Jesus fulfilled His calling from Isaiah 61 to release the captives not just by setting them free, but amidst the process of setting them free, He did what He always saw His Father do: He gave life!

> *Then Jesus answered and said to them, "Most assuredly, I say to you, the Son can do nothing of Himself, but what He sees the Father do; for whatever He does, the Son also does in like manner. For the Father loves the Son, and shows Him all things that He Himself does; and He will show Him greater works than these, that you may marvel. For as the Father raises the dead and gives life to them, even so the Son gives life to whom He will"* (John 5:19-21).

Jesus saw what His Father did at creation. Jesus saw the Father give life to the world, and to humankind, simply by speaking a word. So, is it any wonder that when Jesus began His ministry here on earth He gave new, more abundant life to someone through healing, simply by speaking a word? Is it any wonder He gave life and delivered the oppressed, simply by speaking a word? Is it any wonder that Jesus told His followers that they would do greater things than these (see John 14:12), after His Father had made the same known in regard to the Son's ministry? (See John 5:20.) Jesus picked up the mantle of the Father and used His life and His whole ministry to offer the world the same life-giving power that He always saw the Father operate in. Why would He give anything less? And since we are called to carry the mantle that Christ has left for us, why would *we* give the world anything less?

God is a creative God, and He has never shown us anything to the contrary. He has always given life in creative ways. He led Elisha to use an ax head and empty vessels to reveal the Lord. Joshua and the Israelites were to let out a great shout to topple a massive structure.

God answered Noah and his family with a rainbow of color and promise. Jehoshaphat won a physical battle through praise and worship. The New Covenant Church saw healing come through shadows and handkerchiefs. Jesus used dirt and saliva for healing and turned water into wine! (See Second Kings 6:1-7; Joshua 6:15-20; Genesis 9:12-17; Second Chronicles 20; Acts 5:15; Mark 8:22-25.) Where has our creativity gone? We often live in a black-and-white world desperately in need of colors that our human eye has yet to see. We need new life! We need more life and life *more* abundantly. We live in a world absent of power that needs to see God's nature as Life Giver known and His Kingdom revealed. We have often lost touch, but we were created by and still are within grasp of God's life-giving power. The thief has come all around us and stolen, killed, and destroyed—even in our own lives!

We must pick up the mantle that Jesus took from the Father. As co-heirs with Christ, we must answer and overtake the thief and all the life he has stolen. If we will connect to the Life Giver Himself, He will reveal in us creative colors the world has not seen. And by faith, we can paint the dark, dreary, and oppressed with the fresh, creative, and life-giving word of God! The world is in need of more than we can tell them and is secretly wanting something we, the Bride, can show them.

Oftentimes I would get up and prepare to go out into the heavily populated and hurting streets we lived among in Ethiopia. But before I could be of any positive affect, I had to begin by seeking the Lord's perspective and hearing His voice so that I could see through His life-giving legacy. When I go out into the world each day, or even spend time with my family, I must not just see people as plain sight would show them. I want to see them through God's eyes and see what has been stolen from them or what has been killed and destroyed in their lives. Through my own eyes I may judge incorrectly, but through His eyes I see the injustices the enemy has inflicted upon the Lord's children, and through His voice I hear how to give that life back and how to give it more abundantly.

How amazing it is that God does not just stop at restoring life! His promises go even farther because Jesus does not come just to give or restore life back to where it *was,* but He comes to give life *more* abundantly! Every person and every place where life has been stolen or destroyed is an opportunity to take that ground back and to see each person flourish instead of fall—to see a place where life has been transformed to a place where life is now restored and even overflowing.

The Lord has brought many such needs or opportunities to *"give life"* into our lives, and He has brought them in a variety of ways. Each one has been a lesson for us in how to join the Lord in His mission of releasing the captives (see Luke 4:18) and how to do so through giving life! He is Life, and He is the Life Giver. God has created us with a life-giving power; it is innate within us. He has made this same creative, life-giving power available through us to give and create more for others.

If we will connect with the Life Giver, He will reveal to us the creative, life-giving power that is needed for every situation. He will give birth to new life through our lives and raise up spiritual sons and daughters who carry that life on to many others. He will fill the empty places and breathe life into the dry bones. We will begin to fulfill the mandate from the Garden of Eden to *"be fruitful and multiply"* (Gen. 1:28). If we will give life to those around us, like they are our very own family, we will see the Spirit of adoption come to life (see Rom. 8:15). We will give life, by His Spirit, to *more* family.

The family of God is hurting. Many of the children of God are lost and broken. We, as sons and daughters of the King, must connect to our Father, the Life Giver, and allow His seeds of grace and love to flow through us and give life to the children and the family He has been waiting for. My own family has had one very personal example of this recently.

Our daughter Anna is 13 years old. God gave us the privilege of adopting Anna (previously named Kelemua) from an orphanage home we worked with frequently while living in Ethiopia. It was a small orphanage run by our Ethiopian home church, and it was set up much more like a family home. After we met Anna in July 2007, we met with her almost every week until she officially and miraculously joined our family in January 2010.

During these years, we had a very good, if not great, relationship with Anna while she was at the orphanage. And actually, much of our relationship was built through prayer and time in God's presence together. Our hearts felt an immediate tie to Anna, similar to but in a different way than with our other adopted daughter, Aynalem.

For lack of space, I won't go into our entire adoption story and the miracles God did, as He did a lot. God moved mountains to answer prayers and bring our family together during the whole adoption process. We have much to be thankful for. But the most powerful part of Anna's adventure into our lives came when her relationship with us changed—the day she arrived in our home. God prepared our hearts for some of what would take place, some of which we are still working through. We knew some of the places the thief had stolen from in her life and her past family. But we had no idea of all the relationship challenges that were ahead.

The day Anna moved in, something new began to happen. Her relationship with us started going backward, reversing the course it had been on for more than two years. This happened immediately. Suddenly, right before our eyes, she was drowning in depression. Her attitude and moods of defiance were ones we had never seen in her before. And most difficult of all, Anna was running away from us as parents in communication and relationship. This was no teenage thing; this was a spiritual wound, a "theft from the enemy" kind of thing that began the very moment she moved in under a new authority.

Anna had known us and been very comfortable with us for years, even staying with us at our house for whole weekends with the group from the orphanage home. When told of us being her adoptive parents, she was exceedingly happy and wanted to come. It was her choice. But something spiritual was happening, something from her past wounds and hurts that was trying to yank her back from living new life. And it was stealing much of the life that was already there.

Anna had a very difficult upbringing. She and her sisters lost their parents at a very young age, and she bounced from home to home until God brought her to the Covenant Church Orphanage family. She had been horribly abused: physically, mentally, and emotionally. The abuse came from those closest to her, from those who were in a position of authority, and probably from those who previously had life stolen from them as well. Promises were made to her by many of her caregivers, but they were promises not kept. Every time she might have thought new life was going to be given to her, more was stolen away.

Until she reached the Covenant Church Orphanage home, Anna was losing life by the day. Physically she was moving forward, but in all other ways the "thief" was having his way. God used Covenant Orphanage to restore life to the places it had been taken. Anna found the Lord in the home and discovered an unbridled passion for her King. It's where she came alive. I will never forget the first night eight kids from the orphanage came to stay at our house with us. We went to pray over and say goodnight to each child, but were awestruck when we saw Anna (10 years old at the time) on her face in deep relationship with her Savior. God was restoring life in her, and she was enjoying it as much as possible!

I think this was why we were so surprised at the changes we saw in Anna when she officially joined our family. There was such a strong foundation of the Lord in her from her time at Covenant Orphanage: such character, morals, love, appreciation, and even relationship. But now, it felt like all we had seen restored in her over those years was being stolen away at the threat of moving past the old life and into God's new. We were aware of the changes and difficulties for any child in this situation, and we knew that a patient kind of love was even more necessary than usual. What we found was someone whose past was suddenly present again. Fear brought the thief's previous workings back before her eyes and paralyzed her from moving forward. The thief was trying to steal from her again. This time it came not through reality, but from a fear so strong she could hardly look at us long enough to blink, let alone utter a word in our direction.

In every form of communication, fear paralyzed her from relating to us in the most basic of ways. This was just the beginning, and fear's control over her only seemed to strengthen. On most days, neither my wife, Destiny, nor I could get more than five words from her for the whole day. Maybe a "yes," a "no," or something simple like "good," in response to a question. The moment we became her parents, her fear of rejection began to steal the hope of new life together.

It wasn't about us. We knew she loved us. We knew that deep down she genuinely wanted a relationship with us, probably to the same great extent that the fear controlled her. But she could not move. And no matter how much we tried to help, connect, or patiently love her through this transition, we were met with resistance and avoidance.

It began to get more difficult to watch her build new comfort levels with others and walk right past us each time into their arms. It was hard not to get to love her openly and outwardly, to have that love rejected because she was so afraid of rejection herself. We would pull her aside many times to talk and pray, and we tried a variety of things to get closer, to help us understand, or to help her walk past the line drawn in the sand. Nothing worked. We began to find that now it wasn't just about an inability to connect or have a relationship; now she was beginning to act out in ways we had never seen in her before.

Anna displayed new attitudes and new instances of defiance and rebellion that we did not believe were really her. The bottom line was that she did not know what she was doing, nor could she help it. Over and over we tried to remind her of who God had made her to be and of the love, faith, and light that was in her heart. She agreed, and sometimes we could tell she wanted to try. But each time she would reemerge even further from relationship, deeper in a pit of darkness as if a cloud cover joined her wherever she went. Through this, her tension and frustrations seemed to increase. She was bottled up with what was being stolen from her. She wanted a relationship so badly, but she could not have one due to fear of rejection and her past. So she just kept deciding to reject the relationship to prevent an even worse pain. The cycle was getting deeper, and it was affecting her and our other daughters more and more each day. It was becoming a crack in the family that no effort could fill.

One day the situation at our house was hitting a boiling point. So many difficult and negative things were coming in through this division and through the fear that was present. It was tearing us apart. Anna had so much life being stolen from her that it was now affecting our whole family in a way she couldn't help. She didn't want it to be that way, and we knew she was hurting terribly through it all. But she didn't know what to do and was paralyzed by the thief, his fear tactics and lies. We wanted only to give her life, whatever life the Lord wanted to give her. Instead, we were seeing it stolen away from us all. Every way we tried to give life back to her was met with resistance. We were truly at a breaking point and did not know what to do—only to keep waiting on the Lord to listen for His fresh answer.

The same day the house and family was about to boil over, God gave us revelation. It seemed simple at first, but we had only to be obedient and give it a try. We would trust Him with the results. The Lord spoke to us about using a notebook with Anna to start over in seeking to have a relationship and communication together. We had tried to have her write to us before, but it didn't work. But God put this idea before us, and we had to try by faith. We brought her the notebook and began to reaffirm our love for her, as well as our desire to have a relationship. We told her that we were going to leave this notebook in one place for her, as well as for Destiny and myself. The notebook would be for conversation back and forth, to express the words that could not, would not come out from her mouth. She could tell us anything, ask us anything, even empty her heart if she wanted to. This notebook could be all of our voices, and it could be done safely in her own time. With the way the house and family felt, it seemed like our last shot.

Anna nodded in agreement to the relationship notebook, and we showed her where it would be waiting. After this conversation, we left the room and continued in prayer. I checked back on the notebook a little while later, but there was nothing. Another half hour went by and still no attempt. I had written the first note to her, something very small and simple. I wasn't sure if she even felt safe to seek out the awaiting notebook on her own, so I decided to take the notebook up to her. I went in, and we sat on her bed together. I took the pen and began writing to her while sitting side by side. "Anna, do you want help?" Then I wrote the words "yes" and "no," so she would only have to circle one for an answer.

"Yes," she took the pen and circled it slowly.

"Do you want the fear and the bad things gone?" I wrote in response. Again I finished with the words "yes" and "no," so she could circle her response.

"Yes."

"Will you help try and make them go away?" I wrote next, believing that if she wanted the thief gone from her life, she had to take the authority to tell him to go.

"Yes," she circled.

Then I wrote one last question, a question based on the passage in Luke 11. Jesus says that if we cast out the enemy, but do not continue to take authority over our house, the evil spirit will try and come back the next day with seven more like him to steal, kill, and destroy even more from our lives (see Luke 11:24-26). So I wrote this final question: "If they go away, will you try to keep them away every day?"

"Yes," she circled.

"That is wonderful!" I answered out loud. I actually got a smirk in return. At this time I spoke and asked her if we could have a prayer time later to see God give life back to these places. She nodded yes. I asked her permission for who would be involved in this prayer time, and received it through a nod. Then I left the room and put the notebook back in the place we had agreed upon.

We were almost at the prayer time when I went to check the notebook, just in case. I opened it up and there it was—a full page note to Destiny and me communicating so much of what had been welling up inside of her. Her voice was being stolen from her by fear and her past, but now life was starting to reenter. We couldn't believe what we were reading or even that we were reading something from her at all. A relationship was beginning, and an avenue for new and abundant life was opening up.

We gathered around Anna and took her through several Scriptures in Luke 11 to help prepare her. She had been around prayer times such as these with the church people who ran the orphanage home and also amidst our family. We went over some principles Jesus spoke of, then went into a prayer time of love, healing, and deliverance, and then we all began speaking forth new life! The prayer time went on for more than two hours, and by the end, Anna stood there in the middle of us all full of light, arms outstretched to the heavens and rejoicing before the Lord. She took authority over her life, sent the thief away, and received new life in those places. Anna was beaming, she was singing to the Lord, and we were all ministered to by His presence.

Since this prayer time and the new, unique avenue of relationship and communication, Anna has walked around like a brand-new person. The frustrated and tense demeanor she had shown is now gone. She had been so bottled up with the life the enemy was trying to steal; it had been causing her to act out in ways she never had before. Conversation has yet to take its full place verbally, but she has opened up with full bloom on paper. Every day, morning and night, Anna started writing to us. She began sharing her feelings, her past, her questions, and even her love for us. We have communication now. After more than a year together, there is life in our relationship, and there is life again in and out of Anna.

Within days of life being restored in these places, we found Anna praying freedom and release over several others in need. God was not just giving her life, but through this 13-year-old girl, He was now passing it on to others. The thief tried to steal because that was his entry point to try to kill and destroy life in the family, especially in Anna. But God gave us revelation—revelation that gave life—and opened the door for life more abundantly. God did not just redeem Anna from a hurting or broken place; He grew our family and gave life to a daughter we had not yet been able to know.

The Lord has a simple, creative answer ready for any and every situation where the thief has been or is taking life. God has fresh revelation ready to give us to help breathe life into others in need and grow His family. He has power like a bottled-up dam, waiting to flow through the authority He has given us. But it is not until we remember the testimony of the Life Giver Himself, open our eyes, and listen for His voice that we can know His creative, life-giving power and be ready to pass it on to the person or circumstance in front of us. Our faith will only grow when we remember what a big and creative God we are loved by. All throughout the Bible, God creatively answered the impossible. Just as He used Elijah, Moses, and the disciples before us, God wants to reveal Himself to the world in this same way through us and through His creative, life-giving power.

Today, allow the same creative, life-giving power that has been breathed into you to breathe through you to a world that is gasping for fresh, heavenly air. It can be something as simple as the solution of a notebook for communication, an act of love and service, or a powerful time of healing, deliverance, or prophetic blessing. It may be a specific word of encouragement God gives you for someone you see on the street or an email declaring prayers of faith over a friend in need. Jesus has placed a great opportunity before us, and the devil's thievery only increases our opportunity to join Jesus in His life-giving ways. We must take this opportunity, tap into the Life Giver Himself, and begin to give life more abundantly to all those He has entrusted into our path. Life is waiting! And the whole world is our family in need.

Chapter 1

VISION OF THE PROMISED LAND

SUDDENLY, amidst all of our needs, defying the battles and long odds we were up against, the vision came to life! I was still on earth—still in my own living room for that matter. But my heart, my eyes, and everything within me were in a new place, a heavenly land! I stood there gazing in circles all around me, spinning as if on a turntable. But I was not in a parade, and there was no podium, just fields. It was beautiful and beyond breathtaking. I was surprised by this place, yet at the same time completely engaged. God obviously wanted me to learn something. I breathed in with a deep breath while I tried to set my heart to understand. It was a land of unmatchable freedom, a freedom that was blowing across me like a refreshing wind. And everywhere I looked seemed to surpass anything and everything I knew. It was a land of life-giving promise, *a promised land*.

As far as my eye could see, the land appeared as an orchard, a place of fruit and lush, unmatchable greens. The vision and the promises I had received and believed all these years looked as if they were right before my eyes. "My Kingdom come, My will be done, on earth as it is in Heaven." I didn't know where the voice came from, but I could hear it in my heart as clear as the trumpet will someday sound. What a fruitful land! Full of life!

Am I in Heaven? I had to question. *Is this my eternal land and home?* My feet still stood on earth, so I did not know for sure. But this was just as real, like I was in two places at once. But I knew where I was: I was taking possession of the heavenly answers I would one day live in, the same answers that, for the time being, needed to flow through me to the difficult, and even impossible, circumstances that were in my life and the world around me.

On earth, we were in great need in a variety of areas. We were waiting for answers only God could swoop in and provide. In Heaven, God was showing me the answers: the land I was not only to ask for, but the land I was called to own, use, give, and multiply for His glory. It was as if all our prayers and God's stored up answers were in this "spiritual property" I was just starting to understand. On earth, I was receiving emails, phone calls, and visits every day from those in great need who were standing faithfully or struggling mightily amidst dire physical circumstances. But there—here—in Heaven, not knowing how I was connecting, I was inheriting the answers of God: His fruit to sustain and grow, His milk and honey to bless, and a land I was being given for the direct purpose of seeing it come to life on earth. But how? I felt like a volunteer in a magic act, with my body cut in two and the box separating each half into different places. My feet were on the ground, but from the waist up, my surroundings were beyond description. It was bigger, more divine, and more expansive than I could give credence to. This place was, simply, heavenly.

A PROMISING ENCOUNTER

Just then, a man began walking my way. I was speechless. *Was this who I thought? What should I say?* He reached out his hand as if to shake mine, and instead I reached for a hug. "I'm Adam," he said, without an ounce of prestige. Like a regular ol' guy, he acted as if he was coming to "hang out."

"I know you must have many questions," he spoke calmly. "From the look in your eyes and your mouth agape, you seem a little surprised."

All I could muster was a nod.

"As I believe you are somewhat understanding, this is your promised land. This is a piece of Heaven that God has passed down to you through Jesus. However, this is not only the place for your heavenly dwelling; it is the place you are to operate, live on, and give from for the rest of your time on earth. Your heavenly inheritance, though eternal, must first be used to bring fruit to earth. This land, just as the Lord gave me in Eden, is a land of promise that you are to take dominion over. I lost sight of that. I let self and worldly deceptions creep in to steal my God-given vision and purpose. I had everything I needed in the land the Lord gave me, but I acted as if it wasn't enough to sustain self, let alone pass on fruit and the taste of Heaven to others. I had the opportunity of Heaven on earth in my very own hands, but I missed it. I was given a land like this but did not understand how to use it, how to own it for the benefit of all, or how to harvest it and pass its free and powerful blessing on to others. I was given so much, but I did not recognize what I had been given. This is why you are here. You must recognize what God has given you and do with it what I did not. You must see the purposes and power it holds and learn how to be *of* this land, even while you are still *in* the world.

"Your promised land is not only an eternal home. But neither is it something to be rained down only for your blessing and comfort on earth. You have a promised land that you may take hold of now, by the inheritance of God through the Lord Jesus Christ. It is a land of fruit—lots of fruit—and a land flowing with milk and honey. It is a land where you as a "son" and heir with Christ must take what you own here and make it known, tasted, and distributed on earth as it is in Heaven. You must take this promised land the Father has graced you with and begin to live out a promised life."

I couldn't help but pause while he was talking. I was overwhelmed. Not just by his words, but by looking at all that surrounded me. I saw high, eternally peaking mountains that simply glowed. They didn't just glisten, but had the glow of everlasting life. Rainbows danced through the air like peace and promise had come together for a night at the ball, and the skies were ever reaching. The magnitude of the atmosphere was almost more than I could handle. I was nervous to talk because I felt my lips could do nothing but quiver. "This was, this will be…*is* life more abundantly!"

I must have said the last part out loud without recognizing it because that's when I began to hear Adam speak again, answering what I had unknowingly declared.

"This is life more abundantly. Absolutely! And it will be here waiting for you and many more for many, many years to come. But, if you will recall Jesus' own words, He went down to earth because of the thief who was stealing, killing, and destroying. Jesus came to visit the earth, and all humankind upon it, to give life more abundantly. And while that abundant life will be experienced here someday, it is also meant for earth. God's Kingdom is life more abundantly, and it must be given out through you now—there," he said, while pointing below.

"When Jesus arose from the dead, He rose in a resurrection power that is now within you by the Spirit of God. Truly, you are full of power by the Spirit of the Lord. Jesus rose on earth and went to Heaven so you could take what is of Heaven and remodel, restore, revive, and reform life on earth. He rose with resurrection power, knowing that in Him you would have authority, as the Father gave me originally in the garden: authority to rule, be fruitful, and multiply *His life* on earth as in Heaven. Jesus became a life full of resurrection power, distributed for the sake of all, that none should perish and miss out on the life more abundantly that you see all around you. But, this means that you must not simply partake of this fruit God is giving you. It means that you must not just live in this heavenly land the Father has entrusted to you. It means that you must take what you have freely received here and freely give it there. As the Lord spoke to me, I speak the same to you. Be fruitful and multiply."

More quickly than he arrived, Adam was gone. But I was still there—wherever *there* was. I looked all around, still taking in what surrounded me, still trying to understand this feeling of being in two places at once. I had often heard the phrase that we can be "so heavenly minded that we are no earthly good." I never gave the statement much credit, and this confirmed my opinion. I had to be more heavenly minded, as long as my feet remained on the ground. God was stretching me to experience His promised land now, so my feet could carry me across the earth to take this fruit, this lavish, soothing milk and honey, and give it freely to the world in need. With all the practical difficulties that those on earth were going through, the practical solutions had run their course. We needed Heaven! We needed our promised land now! Earth, and all of God's children across it, were in need of answers that only the fruit of Heaven could give. They had wounds that only the promise of honey could soothe. They had weakness that only the sustenance of milk could supply. This place was amazing, and I could hardly wait to explore and learn more.

I walked over toward the trees to my left, about 20 yards or so. I could see and feel myself in both places at once. It was very odd, an almost indescribable feeling. At this very moment, I could see many of the people and issues around our lives, yet at the same time, I saw the fruit within reach to help answer them.

No longer was I praying from earth to Heaven hoping for a down-pour of answers. No, this was different. Now, I was taking hold of the fruit from my very own trees, from my own promised land I had inherited from my Father. It was fruit filled with answers and with the very life of God Himself. I was simply, with authority, distributing and imparting God's promised fruit over those in need. I wasn't just asking anymore. Now, through prayer, I was co-laboring with God to see His promises come to life, distribute life, and transform life! My prayers were aligning with His grace, and I was giving according to faith. I was releasing the fruit to those in need, giving it as freely as the Lord had just given me. It really was just as Adam had spoken: I was being fruitful, and I was multiplying. However, it was not my earthly fruit or anything I could produce. It was all free! It was all God's, and He had made it available to us. *It had been growing this whole time!* All these years I had been asking for it to come, to fall upon our needs or upon the earth. I realized fruit falls at a much slower rate than it is picked. But taking ownership and having possession of my promised land allowed me to receive freely and give freely.

As I then began to receive this place He had brought me into as my own, I could not help but fall to my knees. The magnitude of what this promised land represented, and the immense stewardship that comes along with it all, was dawning on me. It was a humble privilege, and now even my knees could feel it. They sunk into the strong, recep-tive ground in complete and utter dependence. "With great authority comes great responsibility," I remember hearing that phrase so often over the years. It was a phrase I always tried to live. But never had its words come to life quite like this moment. My Father had not only brought me into a new land, but He had given this land to me. Right then I knew full well that this promised land was not only a promise for me, it was a promise that had to be revealed in Spirit and in Truth through me to the earth below.

I couldn't help but wonder, *How?* My feet were on the ground, and on the ground they had to stay. But my land, God's promises, and the produce of such a land was right before my eyes with full access. *How do I live in the world but not of it? How do I keep my feet on the ground while living by faith from this new land God had given me? How do I steward the fruit of Heaven to answer the yearnings of the Father's family on earth?* However it would happen, I was dependent. That in itself was reassuring. There is no more refreshing feeling than being totally and wholly dependent on Him, yet still empowered to live and give on my own. Something new was beginning. A place I had often longed for was opening up. But how?

TEACH ME HOW!

I dropped further to the ground, from my knees to my face. The soil was so rich and full I could smell it! Who knew that even dirt from the ground could smell so heavenly? The scent of the Father rushed through my veins, and I settled into a peaceful, necessary rest with the Lord. I stretched out my hands ahead of me, still prostrate on the ground. I took another deep inhale, like taking in fresh mountain air, turned the eyes of my heart to the Father, and let go. I could not even pray. I just needed Him. "Father, teach me." I muttered under my breath. It was all I could manage. I needed direction and strength that only God could impart. I needed the parts of God I didn't even know to ask for. I needed…

Suddenly I felt something lift me off the ground! Hands underneath my shoulders lifted me to my feet. "My love is better than wine," whispered its way through my ears, or perhaps my spirit. "My love is better than wine," a gentle voice whispered again. Before I could see who it was, I saw a hand reaching out past me, pointing to what lined the fields just ahead and to the right. It was a vineyard, grapevine after grapevine, like never-ending lines of life. "My love is better than wine," He said again.

I turned, knowing now just who it was. "My Lord," I said with an uplifted smile. His presence caused me to glow—not just His presence, but His nearness.

"My love is better than wine. This is My vineyard, and these are the grapes of grace. They are life-giving in nature and full of My love. My love, in its perfect form, is the freedom and wholeness everyone needs in order to be the son or daughter and the life-giver that I have called them to be. My love is an impenetrable force, like a perfect multi-dimensional sphere, forever surrounding those I love, perfecting My love in them so that they may give it out freely. My vineyard is one of grace, poured out with My new wine. One cannot give life to another if one is not full and, therefore, surrounded by My true and impenetrable love. My life-givers are full of this new wine of love, and they know how to give it to the world around them because they are secure in My love for exactly who they are. They are secure in being My children whom I love.

"This vineyard," He spoke while pointing across the outstretched land it covered, "I want you to take of what is Mine and declare it to the world."

When saying this, He spoke to me with such faith. I received equally as much from the way my Lord spoke to me as from His words. He spoke to me with such confidence and trust. He clearly trusted me and believed in me to steward the best parts of His promises and freely pass them out without measure or condition. He was not just telling me what to do; He was imparting the courage I needed to do it! I had never felt more chosen in all my life.

"What you are feeling and receiving from Me is part of the aroma of My grapes of grace and is the effect of My new wine. I want you to be free. My grace is sufficient to set you free from any and all limits.

See, My child, the limits you have been living under? You have limited the amount of love you think I am allowed to love you with. This has broken My heart. There is no floor on Heaven, nor My promises meant for My children. And there is no ceiling to block you from tasting and giving out the best parts of Me. *I AM a milk-and-honey God!*"

Before I could even realize we had moved on, we were already in a new, amazing part of this land of promise. I obviously never really understood what a land flowing with milk and honey meant. But it was right there, lived out before my eyes, and it was not at all as I expected. There was no river of milk, and I half expected to see honey whisked around on the type of honeycomb wand the cartoon bee uses on Honey Nut Cheerios. No, this was different. It blew away my context of milk and honey, yet the smell of such promises was unmistakable.

"Taste and see that I AM good," the Lord said with such hope. "Taste and see for yourself how deep, how lavish and unendingly expansive My love and promises are for you. Taste and see what life more abundantly really means. Many know the words, but do not know how abundant of a God I AM. I am calling them to live in the world, but to give the life of Heaven to those who are parched, hurting, and hungry. But how can one give life more abundantly if they do not know firsthand how abundant I AM? My love and life cannot be contained in mere words or human understanding. And one cannot live, let alone give, what one does not know. Your ceiling has become My floor, and I never modeled My house with a floor where only drips would spring from Heaven. I made My house open and free, so that as you are one with Me, the whole world would believe in Me and receive My abundant love. Taste and see the life I AM calling you to live in Me. Taste and see what I have brought you up here to know. Taste and see that I AM good."

I reached out and grabbed a piece of fruit. What was funny was the piece of fruit I picked seemed at first to be out of my reach. But without even the slightest strife, grace brought this piece to me. I had never seen fruit quite like it before. It was virtually exploding with what could not be seen, but what the Lord wanted me to taste with Him.

I wrapped my mouth around the fruit and sunk in. It was alive! The fruit juices of Heaven not only filled my mouth and invigorated my taste buds; it dripped excessively down my chin. The only word that gave it fair description was *abundant*. It was sweeter than honey I had known, but it carried the sustenance of a rich, creamy glass of milk. I took another bite from the same piece only to find it overflowed even more than the first time, like the juices were alive and regenerating themselves. The taste was even more powerful! It was even more alive! How was that even possible? When I eat a peach, it shrinks pretty quickly, more so in fact than I usually prefer. But this, this was awesome! It was fruit that kept on giving. Every bite exceeded my greatest, wildest expectations.

For far too long I had expected way too little of God and limited His ability to be bigger than life. I had to know this new life so I could give new life to everyone around me. For too long, I had limited how juicy, full, and abundant His love really is, even when communicated through something as small as one piece of fruit. I looked up, still daydreaming about the abundant taste and capability in this one piece. Only now I wasn't looking at my one piece; I was looking at tree after tree, row after row, orchard after orchard. One piece felt like enough, even more than enough. Yet I could not see as far as His fruit of Heaven reached. And each piece was exploding and overflowing with the sustenance of milk and yet still with the blessing, almost like dessert, of honey.

I looked over and the Lord was laughing. So then I started laughing. "Lord, I have often lived like You are Lord of the beans. I'm sorry." I looked to Him with tears streaming down my face and soul, but I still had a smile on my face that could not be tamed. "Lord, You are a milk-and-honey God! Life! *And* life *more* abundantly! Thank You!"

The honey still trickled from the corner of my mouth. Eating that one piece seemed like I had eaten for four. This one piece of fruit gave me more of a taste of Heaven than any knowledge I had ever gained. Oh, how the world needed *that* taste!

A PARADE OF LIFE

I began to worship the Lord, crying out in every part of me with praise! Suddenly, my new heavenly perspective had joined me down on earth. I was in the middle of an impoverished but crowded street. People lined the streets on each side like they were awaiting a parade of floats. Needs were apparent. Pain and hunger were blatant. The depth of longing was unmanageable for my earthly capabilities. I was in the middle of the street and had to do something. "Lord, help me!" I cried out. I was surrounded by close family and friends who were sharing this worldly impossibility.

I looked up through the heavenly promises and perspective God had just shown me. When I looked back down at my hands, I had one large picnic basket. It was full of bread, the grapes of grace, and the fruit of Heaven that had just been overflowing in my mouth. I was so excited that I just—*started to dance!* I began twirling in praise and thanksgiving. I whirled around in circles from side to side of the street passing out the cherished heavenly provisions as quickly as my hands could grab them. I looked over and my family and friends began to do the same. Their hands were full and a celebration began to break out. Praise and worship filled the air like a celebratory rain quenching a drought. The atmosphere was electric.

The people who were once downtrodden and bound by poverty were now rejoicing. Their weeping turned to joy; their mourning turned to dancing. Our baskets kept refilling and multiplying. There was bread and fruit. Even new clothes and other provisions were suddenly pulled out like a rabbit from a hat, except this was many rabbits from many hats. The multiplication seemed to continue. The people were transformed into children of light. Now they could taste and see how good He is! I remember one man's face, forever ingrained upon my internal sight. He was older and tattered from the years, his face dry and leathery, but he was wearing a giant smile. He let the juices of the milk and honey flow out the corners of his mouth when he erupted with joyful laughter. What joy! We started singing it together:

"Taste…

and see…

that the Lord…

is good to me!"

Over and over we continued to sing in one accord. The life juices of Heaven weren't just in the fruit anymore. They were in us! Our lives, even those once held by poverty itself, now overflowed with abundant life, joy, and the juices of Heaven. Everyone got a taste. Everyone was overflowing. I could taste the promised land just looking at the people who were partaking of this fruit. They were new, transformed, very different people. The people were alive, and their life was abundant! Heaven had invaded earth and I was overtaken. This was merely a taste—but a mighty good taste at that.

Looking up from what had truly become a parade of life, I found the Lord. Suddenly it was quiet, like He and I were in our own personal, vertical tunnel. "Thank Yooouuuuuu!" I cried out, literally sobbing tears of overwhelming thankfulness. "Thank Yoouuuuu! I love You, Lord. I love You, Lord. I luu-uhh-uhh-vvv You, Lord." I continued to whisper out loud. Like yelling a whisper. Like Heaven on earth.

Right then the Lord caught me up to a higher place. I felt like a bird perched on a cloud. I had a true bird's eye view.

"Look there," the Lord said to me. "I want you to remember the way you gave life in that parade. The more life you gave, the more you had. It was not about the food or resources that you were passing out. You were giving life. From your closeness with Me, abiding in My abundant life, you took the life that was Mine and declared it to the world around you. Needs will be met when you give life. Joy will return. As you give life, I will cause that life to manifest in people exceedingly and abundantly above all they could ask or think. I AM the Life Giver, and as you connect with Me and live life more abundantly yourself, you will pass out life more abundantly. The two go hand-in-hand. Live and give! Freely you have received; freely you must give.

"Down there," said the Lord, "are the empty places and the dry crevices that need to be filled, oiled, refreshed, and revived. I look upon the earth and see all that has been stolen, killed, and destroyed from and within My children. I look upon the world and see My lost sons and daughters, many of whom blame Me for what the thief is stealing from them. They are all My children! They have these empty places and dry crevices in their lives, much like the dry bones I showed Ezekiel. So I ask you the same question that I asked him: these who are so empty, so dry, can they live? You have tasted of My life more abundantly, and that is My promised land that is meant for all My kids. To those who are empty and those who are dry, I want them to come back into the life of My family.

"I have died for each of them. I gave My life so that you may give My life. I rose to new life, from the grave to resurrection life, and it is that new resurrection life I want you to give them. To give them life means to give them more than what you have in your hands. You must speak and declare life over them according to My storehouse of Heaven. You have done well to give what you can give. But I am calling you higher. I want you to give that which can only come from Me. You must give from My grace. More than what you have in your life, you must give of what you have in Me. Take of what is Mine and declare it to the world. Take of what you have tasted of Me and speak it, show it, and prophesy it out loud over the empty places and dry crevices of My people. My kids must know what an abundant Father they have. They must know that My love for them reaches beyond the earthly standards of love. My love for them is one only a Father, a family, could give. It is unconditional and beyond religion. My love for them must be shown in a new way. They must know from you the love I gave to you.

"I left Heaven and became as a servant on earth to bring life and life more abundantly. I went from one land to another, no matter the cost. I want you, My Bride, to do the same. I have provided the life and love more abundantly, but who will wrap that love around the broken? Who will venture into the lands of the lost and become lost alongside them just to show them I love them? Who will speak words of life and love over those who are dry, spiritually parched, and wanting? Who will live in this world but give of Mine? Will you?

"Tap into the promises of Heaven and overflow on earth. Keep your head in the clouds, but your feet on the ground. Give life, and give it more abundantly. Give life according to who I AM. Give life from the oneness we share. Give life, give it again, and again, again, and again until that life reaches all My children, all nations, and every generation. You have tasted and seen My abundance. Now, live according to who I AM. I AM the Life Giver, and I have created you to be one, too. I love you."

I understood that I had a calling on earth, but that I had to keep coming back to this place. I had to keep tasting of this heavenly fruit and distributing it on earth as it is in Heaven. The world needed more. More was clearly available. God's definition of life clearly included far more than mine. I had to give life on earth according to Life in Heaven. The parade of freedom God had allowed me to experience was the parade my life was to be wherever I go, whomever I am with.

My life has to be a parade of life, carrying, declaring, and giving out the fruit and life of Heaven to the dry and empty places on earth. No longer could I give out man's version of God and of Heaven. If earth would experience more, I needed more. I needed the "more" parts of God. I needed to reveal Him as He truly is—abundant. Then it will become a family feast of life!

Chapter 2

GIVING LIFE

"*I want My Bride to be the Mother I have called her to be.*" And with that, I was wrecked! Hearing the Lord whisper this burden to me, God broke my heart and woke me up to realize much of what He had us involved in and the movement of love and family that He wants to grow. The Father, like any good father, wants to save and grow His family. And when He looks at us as the Bride of Christ, He sees a Bride who can carry *His* heart to earth. We can do this by living as more than a Bride preparing for marriage, but as the life-giving mother that every bride can truly be.

Now, we often look at church, missions, outreach, and so forth, as ministry, evangelism, and the like. But the Father, He sees His sons, His daughters, and His Bride. He sees all those who are supposed to be sons and daughters, but are currently lost, hurting, broken, and grieving and who, for some reason, believe that they are forgotten or orphans. They are not orphans. God has had His eye on them, chasing each one this whole time.

Statistically speaking, there are more than 160 million orphans in the world. But as far as the Kingdom and family of God are concerned, these orphans are more than 160 million lost and hurting *sons and daughters* who must be redeemed back into the family at all cost. What would you do if you had 160 million of your own children falling further into the gutters of the world each day? To what extent would you go? Would you want a bride who is focused on the wedding ceremony, or would you want a bride already living and loving like a life-giving mother to your children? That's how passionate our Father is about His children. He wants them back. He wants them to know they are loved. And He is looking for His Bride to be the Mother the world so desperately needs.

Depending on how you see the word *orphan,* there may be a lot more than 160 million who need their Father. That number only represents those the world defines as "orphans." But what about the rest of those who aren't in relationship with our Heavenly Father? What about His children who are outside the love of family because of tension with those inside His house? I'm guessing they didn't actually leave the family because of our "Dad." More than likely it has something to do with us. Our Father is broken over His missing kids. Is He a single dad, alone in His tears? Or will we as the Bride of Christ rise up and be the "Mother" Jesus modeled when He rebuked the religious leaders for their wrong priorities in Mark 10:14? He invited all the children up into His lap. It wasn't the leaders that He blessed; it was the kids, His children! This is a great reminder for us that with God it's not about religion, programs, rituals, or our works. With God, it's all about family. We have a Father who is all about His kids! When God called us to be the Bride, He was not thinking only of marriage; He was dreaming of family—lots and lots of family!

I have to admit this was not always my perspective. In the years leading up to marrying my wife, Destiny, and for a couple years after, I wasn't thinking of who God intended to be part of my family. I wasn't thinking of who God might want to use me to give life to. I was thinking of myself. I was still thinking of ministry, but I was thinking of it through my own plans and ideas. I wanted kids, but I also wanted the things or experiences of the world. Thank the Lord He changed my heart! I cannot even fathom what I would be missing out on.

When God planted us in Ethiopia, He was not asking us to build or grow a ministry. He wanted us to grow a family. One by one, He brought people to us: kids who needed to be embraced, children who needed to get off the streets, those who needed family. We arrived in Ethiopia as a family of three and moved into an overly large, empty house. We didn't know what to do with so much space after years in apartments. But we knew God had a bigger plan than we could even dream of.

When we arrived, our supposed "plan" or "vision" was to build a prayer center, a large complex where we could bring in street children, orphans, and other youth to see them empowered by God. But that was only "our" plan. I have nothing against a plan or a vision. I have often been called a planner, and vision is one of my favorite things to dream about with the Lord. Both are essential components of stewarding what God gives us. But we must remain fresh and flexible and make sure each day that we are joining Him, ready to let Him take our plans and make them that much bigger and better.

God had given us a vision, but He still had plans to reshape that vision to give more life than we could plan. God loves to do exceedingly and abundantly above all we could ask or imagine. We might be looking to see a dream or vision come to fruition, but our Father wants to blow those dreams out of the water with more. We simply must remain close and fresh enough with Him to let Him. He is an abundant God. He longs to bring us into that abundant life with Him where our limits crash down like the walls of Jericho and His glorious possibilities suddenly become realities we never dreamed possible.

The first young leader we started mentoring in Ethiopia was Alex. We had met him several times on our trips before we moved to Addis Ababa, and God was clearly beginning something in this relationship. Alex was about 23 at this time and had lived on the streets since he had been abandoned by his mom at the age of 7. God spoke to our hearts to show us that Alex would be a link to what He wanted to do among the kids and on the streets. So I asked Alex if he wanted to start coming over to the house each day for a prayer time. We took time to talk a little, but mostly we got on our faces to wait on the Lord, dream with God, and hear and see what He was doing. This was completely new to Alex, but he embraced it.

After only a few days, Alex came over and said that he was now waiting on God on his own time. But that wasn't all. "God gave me something," he said. "God gave me a verse for you." I was amazed. I shouldn't have been amazed, but I was. Alex gave me a passage from Second Samuel 7, specifically verse 11. The passage is a message to David from God through Nathan.

David desperately wanted to build God a house. Out of his best and most passionate intentions, David dreamed of building God a place to come and visit, somewhere to rest and dwell. But God wanted to exceed that idea, and this is what He spoke to David in verse 11: "...*Also the Lord tells you that He will make you a house.*" The meaning behind the word *house* is "house, household, family, clan; temple, building."[1] As you can see, the word *house* has two meanings. It can mean "temple, building," but it can also mean a "household, family, or clan." David wanted to build God a house, as in a physical structure. But God had a bigger, more far-reaching idea. He wanted to make David himself into a house. God wanted to birth through David a family tree of descendants. He wanted to multiply life through David and give him a "spiritual legacy" type of house, full of sons and daughters, full of family. David had a great idea, but God had a "life more abundantly" kind of idea!

I went to Ethiopia thinking along the same lines David had been. I wanted to build God a house of prayer. But God had other plans. My idea of a house was a physical structure, but God's desire was a family structure. And that is exactly what God began to do. He didn't bring in money to purchase land or a compound. Instead of bricks or cement, God brought people and future family members. The only question was: Would we recognize what God was doing in time to embrace His plan and His vision for family? We had to catch the new wave of what God was doing before it passed us by and allow God to make us a house, a spiritual family that multiplies outward by giving life to others.

A physical structure can be a wonderful and most necessary component to giving life, but we cannot allow the life God has made available to get trapped inside us or within the walls of a physical building. This is where God calls us to His family structure of multiplication. This is where a move of God goes viral in our communities and gets passed down through generations.

By the time we left Ethiopia, our house was full of ten to twenty people on most days. A number of people had come and gone for days, weeks, or months at a time—abandoned babies, college students, family members, orphans, street kids, and many more. God didn't just fill our house; He began to fill our family. God didn't just want our money or belongings; He wanted what was at the root of those things. He wanted my selfishness. He still does. Even now I cannot help but weep over the fleeting selfishness I allow to stay inside. How many family members could fit in the room of my life that I use for self? How many more people could come back into relationship with their Father? The room is not always filled with bad things, but most often they are not things that give life. I must surrender this room in my life more fully so God can use it to give more life.

Jesus promised in John 14:18 that He would not leave us orphans, but He would send His Spirit to us. This promise speaks directly to the Spirit of adoption Paul spoke of in Romans 8:14-15:

> *For as many as are led by the Spirit of God, these are sons of God. For you did not receive the spirit of bondage again to fear, but you received the Spirit of adoption by whom we cry out, "Abba, Father."*

You know what reminds me that God wants—and is gathering—a big family? Look at the wording used: *"For as many...."* God did not say *some* or put any limitation of any kind. He did not say only those who are qualified, those from a particular denomination or social status. He did not refer to a specific age group, nor did He say only those who had all their broken pieces already put back together. No, God said, ***"For as many** as are led by the Spirit of God, these are sons of God."* I believe the Spirit of adoption is hovering over the nations. He is hovering over lost and broken orphans, street children, the wealthy, the lost, the suburbs, and whole nations that He is wooing back to Himself and His family. The Father is broken over His lost and hurting children. The Spirit is hovering and waiting to adopt them. Jesus gave us the example of how to love like family by laying it all down. Now God is waiting for the Bride to collectively become a Mother who gives life to the nations.

If we are truly the Bride of Christ, we must give up the ways of self. We must let go of the days before children. We must return to our First Love and join the Father in loving, gathering, and giving life to a generation of lost sons and daughters who each became our family when we entered into covenant with God. We are the Bride, but God is calling us to love the world like a Mother.

FROM LIVING TO GIVING

I have an incredible wife. I have an amazing mother. I have four incredible daughters and an awesome sister. My life is surrounded on a daily basis with moms and future moms. They give life to me and to many others. They are life-givers! I will never forget sitting behind Destiny, my wife, in the hospital bed when she was pushing and giving life to our first biological daughter, Mercy. I will never forget holding her hand in Ethiopia when our second biological daughter, Galilee, came to join the party. I could not be more proud of her mother's heart toward our children we have given life to through adoption, Aynalem and Anna, or the children we have seen spiritually adopted off the streets in Ethiopia. Destiny went through a natural and God-ordered transition from living life to giving life. I am incredibly blessed by Destiny, not just as my bride, whom I cherish, but as the mother of our children. She physically gave life to Mercy and Galilee, but she has given life to so many more!

Not everyone can give birth to a natural child, and God understands this. In fact, that is only one small part of giving life. For a follower of Jesus, giving life does not have to be a physical exercise. It does not have to be a multiplication of physical DNA. It is a multiplication of the Father's DNA inside of us coming together with the love, gifting, purpose, and testimony He has put in our hearts. Everyone can give life to spiritual sons and daughters; we simply must transition from "living" to "giving." In fact, it is a transition the Lord is calling us to make. Every day that we stand back, the enemy is going after our lost family members to take even more life than they have already lost.

> *The thief does not come except to steal, and to kill, and to destroy. I have come that they may have life, and that they may have it more abundantly* (John 10:10).

The devil is a thief that is coming day and night to steal life, and far too often we are allowing him, if not at times helping him. We are having life stolen from us, from others, and from those God wants to give life to through us. We have loads of the Lord's DNA, blood, and His very own Spirit within us. However, the fact remains that when we are not giving life, this is when it is being stolen. I believe we have two choices in regard to the life God has purposed for us and stored up in us: give it or slowly begin to lose it. This is not to say we lose our gifting, but that when we stop moving forward, giving life and multiplying, we become stagnant and put ourselves in prime position for the thief to try and steal life from us. When we become stagnant, the thief has an easy target, and a desire to keep us there. We are not called to survive the thief, but to counter him and be givers of life.

A bride values living her life until she makes a transition to being one who gives life. This is when self loses its place of priority and that mama-bear mentality of love and protection begins to grow. Being a Bride is only part of our calling, a stepping-stone to transition to the calling God wants His Church to live out as a loving Mother to the world: a giver of life to counterbalance and overcome the thief and his attempts to steal, kill, and destroy from so many. Mama bears don't worry about their own safety when protecting their cubs, though they do have great instincts to discern and steer their extravagant love. They do not worry about their own lives when they stand on those hind feet and roar with the authority they carry. How do they come by this authority? By choosing to live and give life as a mother. They chase breakfast, lunch, and dinner for all their cubs, and they fight on their behalf. Then, when the cubs are ready, the mama bears release them to go out, be fruitful, and multiply. We must use our calling as a Mother-Church to make sure the whole world knows we are not just trying to evangelize them; we are loving them like we would our own. In God's eyes, they are not just lost; they are family.

As a Mother that is the Bride, we are not just talking about our own personal cubs anymore. We are talking about God's cubs. When we entered into that covenant relationship with God, His cubs became our cubs. We are talking about His lost and broken children everywhere. He is calling us, His Bride, to join Him in giving life to a generation that is dying. What would you do if your child was lost or dying? I believe we all know the answer. We would all fight with everything in us to give life to that child, and we wouldn't think twice about it.

The 160 million orphans around the world are not someone else's cubs. Those who are lost and hurting are not just neighbors we invite to church. Each and every lost, broken, or hurting soul all around the world was created to be a child of God. We the Church are to be the Mother to God's children, so we better become that mama bear up on her hind feet, running through our communities and to the nations, scooping up Daddy's cubs and giving them new life in the family again. Stepping out to save is not a sacrifice when you think of it in your own family context. Why should it be any different for us as the Bride in God's family?

AN OFFENSIVE CALLING

The enemy uses his power to deceive us, make us stagnant, and verify our justifications and excuses as to why we can't go and what we can't afford to lose. But the bottom line remains: If we don't give out what God has given us, we become a stationary target for the thief. We may think we are being responsible or protective for a rainy day, but God didn't command us to protect ourselves. In fact, He gives us promise after promise in the Word that He will do the protecting for us (see Ps. 18:2; 23; Deut. 31:6). God promised us a victory. He has promised us that He will play defense. And He has empowered and commissioned us to go on offense. Our calling is not to protect ourselves or our own lives. No, God gave us a command, "Be fruitful and multiply."

Have you ever played a game of freeze tag? As a kid I grew up playing it quite a bit. But until recently, I had not played in a very long time. This time, I found a lot more value in this game than I ever remember. We were in our last couple weeks before leaving Ethiopia. Destiny, the girls, and I went over to the street kids' shelter to take them through a prayer time. We were specifically talking about Jesus' statement in John 10:10:

> *The thief does not come except to steal, and to kill, and*
> *to destroy. I have come that they may have life, and that*
> *they may have it more abundantly.*

As you can probably tell by now, this verse is a central theme of the movement God has given us. Everywhere we walk in the streets, marketplaces, and so forth, we see people who have had the enemy steal life from them, kill dreams and purposes, and destroy relationships and much more. Our goal as believers is to live, move, breathe, and walk like Jesus, giving life to those from whom the enemy has stolen. Going over this thought again with the kids is why we played freeze tag.

For those unfamiliar with the game, freeze tag has a player who is "it" and is able to tag others by touching them. If someone gets tagged, that person must freeze in place. The other players who are not "it" are trying to keep from being tagged and, therefore, frozen. If they are tagged, they must stay frozen until another person in the game who is free comes and touches them and "unfreezes" them. Then they are free to go forward in the game once again. Our game was set up just the same. Destiny and I were both "it." Basically, we told the kids that we were like the "thief" in John 10:10. This left more than 30 kids to run around the compound, stay away from us, and free each other. We told them that they represented Christians.

The game began, and Destiny and I tried to keep up with the 30-plus kids—a very difficult task when facing so many who are free and who have the power to set others free. At most, I think we were able to freeze up to five or six at a time. But then we would turn our backs to try and tag someone else, and by the time we turned back around, the kids who were frozen would have already been set free again, ready to free others. We would have to start all over. After about 15 minutes, we stopped the game out of exhaustion. We were supposed to be the ones getting them, but in reality, the kids' ability to free one another exhausted us and kept victory as an impossibility for us.

What I like about this game is the picture it portrays to us, the Body of Christ. The enemy is trying to "freeze" us. He is using his lies, schemes, and so forth, to steal, kill, and destroy. This often hurts. We have all experienced one form or another of this kind of hurt when some circumstance in life comes and leaves us seemingly frozen. But God has made it so we can still be free.

However, sometimes out of fear of being hurt again, even when we are set free, we freeze ourselves. Instead of running around and freeing everyone else who is stuck or frozen, we stand still, hide away, possibly try and secure ourselves, or even act like we are frozen to avoid really being frozen. Basically, fear, insecurity, what happened in the past, and all the deceptions that go with those things keep us from playing our necessary part in the game. The more we see others get frozen, the more tentative we become, and the thief starts to take more ground. We forget that we have the power to help give life back to those who are frozen, and slowly we eliminate our dashes of faith to give life to a friend or a stranger, and we miss out on the victory we *all* could have had.

If we as believers stay on the offensive, however, the enemy has no chance. When the thief reaches toward a friend on our right, we give life to the friend on our left. When he chases a passerby, we then impart life to the person on our right who can then go on to multiply to others. Even if we do get tagged, we know the Lord is sending others to our side to give life back to us, leading us back into the game where we can give life to others. As believers, we must not ever choose to stand still or freeze ourselves. We must keep moving forward by faith to give life to those all around us. The victory is assured if we keep playing on offense, if we keep giving life more than we protect our own. We must abandon the ways we protect self, and step out to give life to those frozen all around the world. There will be a multiplication in one direction or another: those who are being frozen by the thief will multiply, or those who are setting one another free will multiply by giving life. Let's move forward and multiply life!

"Be fruitful and multiply..." (Gen. 1:28). This is the command God gave to the first couple He brought together: to be fruitful and multiply. It required a coming together, and as they came to each other there would be a natural reproduction that would bear fruit and multiply the life God had put within them each. As the Bride of Christ, we are no different. We must look to this original command and understand what is possible when we as the Bride of Christ come near to our First Love. When we let go of our own pursuits to come back to Him and His will, we as the Bride will become a Mother. We will have the life that is in us extracted by the Father and mixed with His DNA, and the fruit of such will cause life to flow into others and spread more new life. We have a Father who loves children! He wants sons and daughters. He wants His own, and He wants to gather all those who are lost and without family. He wants a Bride who will be near Him, give life with Him, and gather those whose lives are broken and in need of new life.

I do not believe for one second that God's command to "be fruitful and multiply" was only speaking to natural reproduction. I believe it is a command and mandate from God to always allow and encourage the life within us to keep giving, never stop reproducing, and never stop multiplying. As His Bride, we have spiritual life within us that dies when it is not given toward reproduction and multiplication. It is in our DNA not just to be a Bride, but to be a Mother who steps toward the Father's children. Some of the Father's children are already in the house. Some are lost, and many around the world are so broken and hurting that we must take a Mother's notice.

As a Mother, should we as the Body allow one of God's chosen sons or daughters to go without? Should we see them any differently than we see the very children we have given life to naturally? Should we not step toward His lost and broken children like they are our own family? There is life inside of us. We must make a choice to step forward by faith and let that life inside us collide with the life and the love of the Life Giver Himself. Then we will see what it truly means to "be fruitful and multiply."

REDEEMING FAMILY: BECOMING A BOAZ

The Book of Ruth is often associated with the term *kinsman redeemer*. It is a story about redeeming family. Most of the time, when we talk about the two family members this book focuses on, we quickly go back to Ruth and Naomi. But when it comes to our choice of living life for self or giving life to others around us, there are two other figures we must study and learn from: Boaz and the "other relative."

With all that Ruth had gone through, she was a picture of the poor and broken of the world. She was a picture of our calling in James 1:27:

> *Pure and undefiled religion before God and the Father is this: to visit orphans and widows in their trouble, and to keep oneself unspotted from the world.*

Ruth was a widow, and in the world's terms she was in a great amount of trouble. She was incredibly poor and was without an income. Then Ruth went with Naomi and returned to Bethlehem, a familiar region to Naomi. They returned to Bethlehem at the time of the barley harvest, and according to the law, the owners of the harvest fields were required to allow the poor, the broken, the widows, the strangers, and the orphans to "glean" from their harvest fields. To *glean* essentially meant that they could have the corners, the edges, and the scraps that fell to the ground.

Ruth went out to glean on behalf of Naomi and herself. She found herself in a part of the field owned by Boaz, a relative through Naomi's late husband and a wealthy, well-respected person of the community. To me, this is where the story gets interesting.

When Boaz saw Ruth come into the field, he could have just seen her as one more of the poor or broken who had come according to the law to glean from his field. But instead, Boaz inquired who this young woman was. When he heard she was the daughter-in-law of Naomi, everything changed. Because now Boaz did not just see Ruth as the poor; he saw her differently. Boaz saw Ruth as family!

This is a very important note. How many other field owners would take the time to see Ruth differently? How many would only view her as the poor who should be taken care of by law? Not Boaz.

> *Then Boaz said to Ruth, "You will listen, my daughter, will you not? Do not go to glean in another field, nor go from here, but stay close by my young women. Let your eyes be on the field which they reap, and go after them. Have I not commanded the young men not to touch you? And when you are thirsty, go to the vessels and drink from what the young men have drawn"* (Ruth 2:8-9).

Ruth was so surprised to be cared for to such a level, even knowing that Boaz was a relative. She did not expect to be seen or favored in such a way.

> *So she fell on her face, bowed down to the ground, and said to him, "Why have I found favor in your eyes, that you should take notice of me, since I am a foreigner?" And Boaz answered and said to her, "It has been fully reported to me, all that you have done for your mother-in-law since the death of your husband, and how you have left your father and your mother and the land of your birth, and have come to a people whom you did not know before. The Lord repay your work, and a full reward be given you by the Lord God of Israel, under whose wings you have come for refuge"* (Ruth 2:10-12).

Boaz did not see Ruth just as a foreigner, a widow, or the poor. Boaz saw her heart, what God had put inside of her. Boaz saw what God's response would be toward her as someone who needed to be embraced. He did not only respond to her according to the law of how to respond to the poor; Boaz responded to her as he would toward a family member, with love and favor. Ruth was not only allowed to glean from the fields, but he gave her protection and the freedom to drink freely and to eat at the table in his house. He even told his laborers to let grain fall from the bundles of the harvest so she could glean from the best parts. This always amazes me! Boaz went above and beyond; he gave freely to Ruth and embraced her as family long before she was "officially" a part of his family.

Ruth was given such love and favor from Boaz that under Naomi's direction she went back to him, citing the fact that they were close relatives, and asked to be taken in by him for marriage. We are told that she handled each step properly and virtuously. This was not a grab for money or prestige; Boaz himself recognized that she did not go after man or riches and that she should be blessed for how she handled herself (see Ruth 3:10). Ruth called on Boaz as a close relative, giving him the privilege of taking her in as his own. Boaz acknowledged this role he held as her family and the opportunity this role gave him to step toward her in a powerful and covenant way:

> *Now it is true that I am a close relative; however, there is a relative closer than I. Stay this night, and in the morning it shall be that if he will perform the duty of a close relative for you—good; let him do it. But if he does not want to perform the duty for you, then I will perform the duty for you, as the Lord lives* (Ruth 3:12-13).

To me, this is one of the most unrecognized but most important parts of the story. We often talk of Ruth and Naomi. We include Boaz and the incredible way he stepped with the Lord toward Ruth. But we often miss out on this important decision and the lesson we can learn from the "other relative," who was actually an even closer family member to Ruth than was Boaz. Boaz went to the other relative, shared the truth of the circumstance and need, and then gave the other relative the chance to respond.

> *And the close relative said, "I cannot redeem it for myself, lest I ruin my own inheritance. You redeem my right of redemption for yourself, for I cannot redeem it"* (Ruth 4:6).

The other relative's response breaks my heart. This does not hurt just because of the chance he missed with Ruth. What breaks my heart is how often we as the Church, the Bride, make the same choice that this "other relative" made—often for the same reasons.

The "other relative" saw Ruth and Naomi's situation as one that he feared could be harmful or even ruin his own life and inheritance.

What could he lose if he stepped toward Ruth? She was poor and a foreigner. What might happen? How would he be looked at? What might it cost him?

Ruth is a perfect example of the poor, the broken, and the outcast around the world. We often take it as law to allow such to glean from our fields and do what is necessary to help them survive, just as the other relative may have been willing to do. But when it comes to embracing them in a new, challenging, and even life-giving way, we often tend to look at what we might lose rather than what God is prepared to gain.

The "other relative" saw Ruth as the poor, the widow, and the foreigner and probably would have done what was his duty according to the law. But Boaz saw Ruth differently: He saw her as family. Once Boaz saw Ruth as family instead of just as poor or needy, this godly, fatherly perspective caused Boaz to respond to Ruth differently. He did not just allow her to glean from the corners, but he gave her free privileges to drink, be protected, eat at his table, and glean from the best parts of his work. He embraced her not as one might give to the poor or make a tithe of 10 percent. He lived out the command Jesus later spoke of in Matthew 10:8, *"…Freely you have received, freely give."*

Boaz did not just give freely in the context of money or goods. Boaz gave of himself. In the world's terms, he risked his inheritance to step toward those whom God deemed as family. When the other relative bypassed the chance to step toward Ruth, Boaz took this step with faith. Ruth became his wife, they came together, and through them God gave life to a child. Their child's name was Obed. Later on, Obed had a son. His name was Jesse. Some time after that, Jesse and his wife gave life to another son, David. And it is through the life and line of David that we saw Jesus Christ Himself birthed into this world because God had such a love for us, His lost family.

Boaz did not worry about what he might lose of self in stepping toward Ruth. He only saw one whom God held dear as family. Not only did Boaz not lose anything in taking this step of faith toward Ruth, but Boaz gave life and *gained* an inheritance of life. Like David, God made Boaz a house. The life Boaz gave in stepping toward Ruth is the life we are still living in and through Christ today and the life we will continue to live for eternity. As the "kinsman redeemer," Boaz is often referred to as a "type of Christ" in the Scriptures. Boaz lived *beyond the law* and lived with a grace that was previously unknown in his time. *That* is why Boaz is a "type of Christ." Because he lived out the same calling you and I are commissioned for today: to live beyond the law and with a grace that, unfortunately, has become too widely unknown in our time.

God, the Father, sees all the lost, poor, and broken lives all over the earth. But God does not just see them as the poor, He sees them as sons and daughters, as family! He is waiting for us to rise up as a spiritual Boaz, who gave the kind of love, care, and outpouring toward Ruth that only a family member would give. Too often and too long we have responded to God's children as the other relative did toward Ruth. Ruth shows us a picture of the life God has within the poor, the widow, the orphan, the lost, and the broken—life that is ready to be redeemed and multiplied. God is not calling us to them just to help them survive, but to give life to them so that the same life that flowed out of Ruth and changed the world might flow out of today's global generation of lost and broken souls.

Ruth is scattered all around the world. God is raising up a Boaz that is the Church. *We are Boaz!* We must live and give as Boaz who is a type of Christ who lives beyond the law and shows the world abundant life through abundant love and unusual grace. We must see God's lost and scattered children around the world differently. We must not see them according to the law, but according to the New Covenant of Spirit and grace! We cannot only respond to them as the poor and let them glean from our fields. We must take a large step of faith toward those in our neighborhoods and our nations whom God sees as our family, give the life that God has placed within us, and watch the line of multiplication the Father releases to change the world.

Reflecting back to when we started this story, James 1:27 says this:

> *Pure and undefiled religion before God and the Father is this: to visit orphans and widows in their trouble, and to keep oneself unspotted from the world.*

The Church, as the Bride, is called to what we now refer to as "pure and undefiled religion." But, it has not always been called *religion*. Religion began under the name *covenant*. We are the Bride, called to be a Mother, in covenant with our Lord. We are called to join the Father by stepping toward His children, our own family. We are called to step toward them the way Boaz stepped toward Ruth, with a redeeming love. We are called to give new life to a scattered, broken, and lost generation of God's children. We are called to take the life the Father has given us, love them beyond the law, step toward them, and give life to a new and growing family photo.

The world must know that we the Church are not just a bride, but the Bride of Christ. And we are not only waiting for our wedding day, but we are living here and now, in the world, beyond the law with the kind of love and grace only a mother could give. To reveal God's creative, life-giving power to the world, which is fruitful and multiplies, we must be the Mother God has called us to be.

ENDNOTE

1. James Strong, *Strong's Exhaustive Concordance of the Bible,* Hebrew #1004.

Chapter 3

THE
LIFE GIVER

GOD is my Life Giver. It's probably safe to assume He is yours, too. Going back to the time when God gave me life, my mom was not supposed to be able to have children due to a physical limitation. Having children was one of her and my dad's greatest desires and most fervent prayers. But no matter how much my dad and my mom wanted children, it was not happening. It was an amazing miracle then when God healed that place in my mom so that God could give life through my parents. That was when He first gave life to me, but it was certainly not the last time. He gave me life through an impossible situation. And though God used my mom and my dad to bring that life about, He was and is my Life Giver.

After waiting a long time and through impossible circumstances to have children, my parents were both extremely excited for the life God was bringing forth. They were devoted and incredible parents even before I arrived. The nurses could not kick my dad out of the delivery room. Instead, they were forced to give in to his insistence for a large set of hospital scrubs. He would not let me leave the room without him, for God had birthed new life, and my dad was going to hover over my crib for every last second. You would have almost thought he was the life-giver, but he was simply, and powerfully, one who co-labored in the giving of life.

There was One much bigger, much more powerful, with an even larger Father's heart who was hovering overhead and giving life. Some years later, my dad and mom prayerfully wrote me a blessing for my 16th birthday, one that truly gave me new life! However, that's for another chapter. But that blessing includes a paragraph that directly reflects on the Life Giver and His creative ways, much more than the birth of a child.

> *Joey, I also bless you because you have high value to me. It was learning that you were on your way into this world that helped me turn my life back toward God. I wasn't living a life that honored God at that time, and the news that you were coming really influenced me for the better. And frankly, Joey, you've been making me a better person ever since.*

My dad was in the media industry, and though he had known the Lord most of his life, he had been led astray for a time. Still holding the Lord in his heart, rebellion was driving him farther away from the life that God was calling him to. But when he learned that God had given them the life of a child, not only was there new life being formed within my mom, but new life was rising up within my dad.

My parents co-labored with God to give me life, but God was the Life Giver and was giving life in many more directions than my birth. At that time, my dad left the path he was veering toward and returned to the Lord. He returned with vigor and never looked back. Within a couple years, he received and stepped into God's calling to full-time ministry. He spent the rest of his life traveling the world, crying God-sized tears of compassion, while giving incredible life to many others. God was re-revealed as the Life Giver in my dad's life at my conception and during the miracle within my mom. And through such, He became my Life Giver as well.

HOVERING OVER US

It may have been my dad who was hovering over me for every roll of the crib through the hospital, and he may not have taken his scrubs off for a week, but I was not the only one receiving new life at my birth. God was doing something much bigger—the Life Giver always is. He did a creative miracle in healing my mom, put new life and health in her, caused my life to spring up, gave renewed life to my dad, and then used my mom's healing to birth yet another life in my sister. This one creative, life-giving miracle of God is still multiplying to this day in more ways than we can even imagine. He is the Life Giver, and even before conception, He was hovering over each of us.

> *In the beginning God created the heavens and the earth. The earth was without form, and void; and darkness was on the face of the deep. And the Spirit of God was hovering over the face of the waters* (Genesis 1:1-2).

Many people need a new start—perhaps you or me or someone God puts in our path even today. Sometimes life in this world catches up to us; the world and its ways begin to take over, and we begin to dry up. We need a new start! We need fresh life breathed into us again! Any one of us, or anyone around us, may feel just like the world at its conception: dark or depressed, empty or without form or purpose. That's the glass-half-empty version. But personally, I am an opportunist. And the glass-half-full perspective says that just like the world at creation, just like my dad in the hospital, the Spirit of God is hovering over us as well! God is always ready to bring about new life; we just have to be ready to receive it and ready to pass it on. God is the Life Giver. We must learn to be one as well. We must know the

Life Giver Himself, not just to know how to give life with Him, but how to be so full of the life He gives that we overflow life on earth as it is in Heaven.

HE HAS LIFE: IN HIS VOICE

Then God said, "Let there be light"; and there was light. And God saw the light, that it was good; and God divided the light from the darkness. …Then God said, "Let there be a firmament in the midst of the waters, and let it divide the waters from the waters." Thus God made the firmament, and divided the waters which were under the firmament from the waters which were above the firmament; and it was so. …Then God said, "Let the waters under the heavens be gathered together into one place, and let the dry land appear"; and it was so (Genesis 1:3-4,6-7,9).

Do you sense a pattern in this passage? A powerful and faithful series of events is taking place. Every time God speaks, something happens. After He spoke, life was given to that which He spoke. And each time life sprang forth from God's voice, He saw it through to completion. He saw that it was good, perfect, and without lack. In fact, ten times in chapter 1 we read, *"God said."* When God was ready to give life, He used His voice. God has life in His voice. There is authority in God's voice. He is like a General in command of His troops: When soldiers hear their superior officer speak, they rise to the occasion. The world jumped into alignment every time God spoke. Every time He declared life, life appeared. Even today, the Life Giver still speaks. He hovers over us speaking life. Are we listening? Are we springing up and bearing the fruit of His voice? God's Word never returns void, and His fresh word waits to be received.

...That He might make you know that man shall not live by bread alone; but man lives by every word that proceeds from the mouth of the Lord (Deuteronomy 8:3).

The Life Giver has not stopped speaking. For me, one of the most important parts of this promise is that we see the word *proceeds* in plural, present tense—as in still happening and will continue to happen. It does not say *proceeded*. In a very strategic and life-giving way for us, we live by the words that continue to proceed from the mouth of God. Even more than food, which we have a hard time living without, we cannot be without the fresh and living word of God that continues to proceed from His mouth. We must not live only from what He spoke yesterday or from the vision or hope He gave us last year. We live by the fresh, revelatory word of God that continues to proceed into our spiritual belly and give life to us and others each day. The voice of God offers creative, life-giving power into and through our lives. He speaks, we receive, and then we join Him by freely giving out the yield His voice sowed into our lives.

THE ROOT OF DAVID

There are a number of reasons David was so affectionately referred to as "a man after God's own heart." I believe one of those reasons stems from the fact that David spent so much time inquiring of the Lord. I am convinced that this is why David's life had such life-giving fruit. I can find no one in Scripture outside of Jesus Himself who spent more time, or more occasions, inquiring of the Lord. David opened himself up to the life-giving voice of God, not just once, but daily. God's voice filled David's life and spilled over into all we know today of David's life. We are richly blessed by David's writing, his worship, and his example. Why? David inquired of the Lord and received His fresh, life-giving power. And this lifestyle set him apart. The following psalm of David reflects his own understanding and love for God's voice.

> *The voice of the Lord is over the waters; the God of glory thunders; the Lord is over many waters. The voice of the Lord is powerful; the voice of the Lord is full of majesty. The voice of the Lord breaks the cedars, yes, the Lord splinters the cedars of Lebanon. He makes them also skip like a calf, Lebanon and Sirion like a young wild ox. The voice of the Lord divides the flames of fire. The voice of the Lord shakes the wilderness; the Lord shakes the Wilderness of Kadesh. The voice of the Lord makes the deer give birth, and strips the forests bare; and in His temple everyone says, "Glory!" (Psalm 29:3-9)*

I am moved by the power, the reverence, and the affection David ascribes to the voice of the Lord. He describes it as a life-giving force, one that makes Lebanon and Sirion skip like a young wild ox. I don't know about you, but I don't skip unless I am full of joy and life! My daughter once asked me, "Why don't we skip everywhere instead of walking?" We laughed and tried to offer her a "sophisticated" answer. But then realized we ought to at least try her suggestion instead. So there we were, skipping down the street as a family. You know, there is a lot more bounce in your step when you skip. It truly is an expression of new and renewed life! And when I think about it, I think she was right. We should be skipping everywhere that we go. It would go a long way toward revealing the life inside of us, the life wanting to overflow us, and the life that is being spoken into us by His voice. Come to think of it, I can remember quite a few times I felt the strong urge to start skipping down the street, all because of hearing the Life Giver's voice speak something fresh to my heart. When the Holy Spirit illuminates something fresh from His Word in my heart, it's all I can do not to skip up and down the street. It's not excitement alone that makes us want to act so oddly; it's that when God speaks He imparts new, fresh, heavenly life into us. His voice gives life, enough to make us want to skip—even in public!

David goes on to say that *"the voice of the Lord makes the deer give birth."* David realizes that God's voice births new life, just as it did at creation. Not only does it make the recipient want to skip down the street, but through birth it brings forth multiplication. The voice of the Lord does not only give life to us, but it gives life through us. It is like a father and mother to a child. The Father puts the seed of His voice within us, and if we receive it and nurture the life-giving word He has fed us with, that seed from His voice will mature through a process and come out as new life.

David knew the power of God's voice. So, is it any wonder that Jesus Christ, coming from the Life Giver, came to give life *more* abundantly on earth through the *"root of David,"* one who had learned how to receive the life-giving power of God's voice? (See Isaiah 11:1; Revelation 5:5.) David's love and reverence for the voice of God not only caused him to receive fresh life within himself, but it caused him to be a root of "life more abundantly" being birthed and given to the world. If we want to know the Life Giver, we must know His voice.

HE HAS LIFE: IN HIS FACE

Have you ever looked into someone's face and said, "I want what they have!"? Was there a time you were down, maybe even slightly depressed during a day, and you ran into someone who brought you joy, immediately affecting your mood and demeanor? Has someone else's smile ever caused you to smile? Our faces are very powerful things. More often than we know, we give out more than words simply by our facial expressions and countenances. In what may seem like small ways, we affect others every day through our face-to-face contact. Looking into someone's face is something we do so frequently and commonly that we forget just how big an impact it has upon our thoughts and our actions. The expression of one's face brings to life much of what is inside and can offer a tangible, powerful expression of joy, light, and love.

Recently, I met a new group of boys from the street in Addis Ababa, Ethiopia, for the first time. There were six of them with us that day, and as our time progressed, I began to ask them a few questions. One of the questions I asked was, "What makes you happy?" They went all around the circle with various, although somewhat typical, answers. Then one of the boys gave an unexpected answer: "I'm happy when I saw your face come up the stairs."

"Really, why is that?" I asked.

"Because you looked so happy to be here and that made me happy." What a humbling response to take in and a great reminder for me to have that same joy all the time. He could see the love Jesus has for him, and he could feel the love of Jesus coming toward him just through my face! And the best part of all was that he saw something that did not need any words to be spoken. Without even knowing the reason I was there, the joy of the Lord pushing its way through my face began to change him and make him "happy!"

> *In the light of the king's face is life, and his favor is like a cloud of the latter rain* (Proverbs 16:15).

I find this particular word of the Lord so rich that my heart goes "whoa!" every time. There is so much potential in this word. More than we can even comprehend, I suspect. From its outer appearance, we read that there is a promise of life in the king's face. But then we realize that the Scripture is not just referring to God our King, for the words *king* and *his* are both started with lowercase letters. So this tells me that the light of *any* king's face has life to give. That's where my mind gets excited. If there is life to be found in the light of any human king's face, what more is waiting to be found in the face of the King of kings Himself? If a child can be made "happy" when looking at my face, what if that same child learns to seek the face of Life Himself? Now that thought is a dream come true for me. The face of God, our King of kings, is waiting to be sought out, and in His face there are rivers, wells, and oceans of untapped abundant life ready to be poured out and revealed to a parched world. God is looking for people who will be pipelines of life. He is looking for people who will seek His face, connect to the life, joy, and light within Him, and reflect that life from His face to the world.

> Now it was so, when Moses came down from Mount Sinai (and the two tablets of the Testimony were in Moses' hand when he came down from the mountain), that Moses did not know that the skin of his face shone while he talked with Him. So when Aaron and all the children of Israel saw Moses, behold, the skin of his face shone, and they were afraid to come near him. Then Moses called to them, and Aaron and all the rulers of the congregation returned to him; and Moses talked with them. Afterward all the children of Israel came near, and he gave them as commandments all that the Lord had spoken with him on Mount Sinai.
>
> And when Moses had finished speaking with them, he put a veil on his face. But whenever Moses went in before the Lord to speak with Him, he would take the veil off until he came out; and he would come out and speak to the children of Israel whatever he had been commanded.
>
> And whenever the children of Israel saw the face of Moses, that the skin of Moses' face shone, then Moses

*would put the veil on his face again, until he went in to
speak with Him* (Exodus 34:29-35).

Look at the shining face of Moses in this passage. I do not mean
just read about Moses' face in this story, but truly look at it! Imagine
how you would be affected if you come into church one week, and as
you enter the building, your pastor is standing at the door greeting
each person. But you have never seen him like this! You walk up to
your pastor, but you cannot even shake his hand for looking at his
face. This week, unlike any other, your pastor is glowing. He has spent
so much time in the presence of God, seeking His face, that now He is
glowing with the glory of the Lord. Wow! Would you even be able to
hear the words from his sermon? Would it even matter at that point?
Or would you be so consumed by the glory of the Lord shining from
his face that you would spend the whole service daydreaming about
what happened? You would wonder what was different in his life to
cause such a glow. Possibly, hopefully, you would even want that same
glow and same complexion for yourself. There is something about
seeing life in someone's face that makes you want it, too.

People put all sorts of different creams on their faces to preserve
life or create the image of more life by looking younger. Many consumers become intently focused on their complexions—just look at
the number of commercials or ads. My wife loves her face lotions,
masks, toners, and so forth. I can't say I know enough about what
each one does, but the results are great. She will gladly trade any of
her favorite body care products for those that have the same effect on
her face. She cares about her complexion, just as most of us do. Our
own face is often the first thing we see each day. Every time we look
in the mirror or someone approaches us, it is the life in our faces that
is immediately on display.

As consumers, we spend millions on products to give life to our
faces. But what if we realized we can receive that life in our faces for

free and that it is a multiplying, "pass-it-on" kind of life? Like a coupon for "buy one, get as much as you want free." In the light of our King's face, there is abundant life. And when we are face to face with God, He changes our complexion and gives us a youthful light and a powerful glow. He wants to change our complexions to mirror His, to make our faces walking advertisements for His life-giving nature. He wants to bring new life to our faces—life that does not just spread by word of mouth or advertisement, but through face-to-face contact.

When I read about Moses I always say, "I want what he had!" Many of us hear about Moses and perhaps pray for the very same glow from time to time, but do we really believe we can possess it? Can we glow like Moses did? Can we get that close to God? Do we live and seek His face like it really and truly is possible? In my own case, I sure don't do it enough. I want more, and more is found in His face.

Our doubt often takes us away from the glow available to us. But in fact, we have an opportunity for an even greater glow because He has called us to a greater glory. The veil has been lifted, and the glory, with its residual glow, is waiting. Bill Johnson offers some of the best teaching on this subject that I have heard or read. So I would encourage you to check those teachings out for yourself.[1]

But we find that the greater glow is indeed possible because of the greater glory told to us in Second Corinthians 3:7-18.

> *But if the ministry of death, written and engraved on stones* [Old Covenant], *was glorious, so that the children of Israel could not look steadily at the face of Moses because of the glory of his countenance, which glory was passing away, how will the ministry of the Spirit* [the New Covenant] *not be more glorious? For if the ministry of condemnation had glory, the ministry of righteousness exceeds much more in glory. For even what*

was made glorious had no glory in this respect, because of the glory that excels.

For if what is passing away was glorious, what remains is much more glorious. Therefore, since we have such hope, we use great boldness of speech—unlike Moses, who put a veil over his face so that the children of Israel could not look steadily at the end of what was passing away. But their minds were blinded. For until this day the same veil remains unlifted in the reading of the Old Testament, because the veil is taken away in Christ. But even to this day, when Moses is read, a veil lies on their heart. Nevertheless when one turns to the Lord, the veil is taken away.

Now the Lord is the Spirit; and where the Spirit of the Lord is, there is liberty. But we all, with unveiled face, beholding as in a mirror the glory of the Lord, are being transformed into the same image from glory to glory, just as by the Spirit of the Lord.

There was glory in the Old Covenant, but we are called to much more glory now, beyond the veil! This is not a new teaching, but for many of us it remains a new place to actually venture into. I don't just want to know the Word; I want to live it in every way possible. We have to go there and believe in the greater glory made available to us through Christ. We must seek His face with faith and let Him give us a greater glow in the process. Moses received life when He sought the face of the King. Today, even more life is available to us. We seek out the age-defying, life-giving creams and lotions, why not seek the face of the King Himself?

Is it any wonder the Lord spoke to Moses and gave him the priestly blessing to pass on?

And the Lord spoke to Moses, saying: "Speak to Aaron and his sons, saying, 'This is the way you shall bless the children of Israel. Say to them: "The Lord bless you and keep you; the Lord make His face shine upon you, and be gracious to you; the Lord lift up His countenance upon you, and give you peace"'" (Numbers 6:22-26).

Both the shine on the face of the Lord and His countenance upon our faces are life giving, multiplying encounters. Moses was not just giving this blessing with words; it was a living testimony in his life. He had experienced the shine of God's face. He had an authority through personal testimony to pass it on. God's face gives us life, and that life is transferred through us to give new life and more life! It is very powerful simply to offer this blessing to others, but imagine that your face is shining with the glory of the Lord when you offer it to them. We can do more than just tell people a promise that is available; we can speak it over them while showing them the very life we have received from the King. The result would be undeniable, and the Life Giver would be seen.

The face of God is a life-giving force. It gives life to us, and this kind of life is constructed so that it passes on freely, easily, and powerfully. Seeking the face of God is one of the quickest ways to find new life. It changes your complexion more than any age-defying cream ever could, and it leaves a product that lets you pass on this new life for free.

My younger sister, Jackie, and my dad used to have their own little battles for who was "king" of the house. She wanted authority at a very young age. This really is not who she is now, but even she would admit to the battles back then when she was very young. One of the more friendly battles they had for superiority was a face-to-face staring contest. This was also a way they spent time together, playing unique games such as these. Jackie would seek out my dad and ask him for a duel, to which he would almost always comply. My dad was king of the house (a title she wanted), and she knew she had to go face-to-face with him for even a shot at walking in the authority she wanted. She was very good at these staring contests, often coming out the victor. She didn't always know how to focus and stare like this, but she learned quickly from our dad once the games began. She saw the expression of determination on his face, and it fed into her. The more she stared into his face, the better she got. She wanted authority, she went face-to-face with the king, and she absorbed what she saw or experienced. To this day, Jackie can give a pretty firm stare.

It is time for us to have a staring contest with God. Perhaps with a slightly different intent than my sister had, but He is the Life Giver, and in His face there is life. By playing this game, we put ourselves in position to learn from Him, to receive from Him, and even to carry the authority we must operate in to give life with Him. If we will walk in the authority presented to us to be life-givers, we must go face-to-face with the Life Giver Himself. We have to seek Him out and absorb His expressions, His love, His light, and His glory. We need to go to our Father, the King, and get some face time. We need to carry the greater glow promised to us within His greater glory. We need to see and understand His smile, until that is the smile that we give to others. We need to see His tears so that we cry for the same things. We need to know His joy so we can overflow to the world. We need to have a staring contest with God. *In the light of the king's face is life, and his favor is like a cloud of the latter rain*" (Prov. 16:15).

HE HAS LIFE: IN HIS GRACE

Many of us are aware of the Tree of Life God put in the center of the Garden of Eden. But are we aware of the new "family tree" of life that God began with Abraham? *"In your seed all the nations of the earth shall be blessed, because you have obeyed My voice*" (Gen.

22:18). With Abraham, God planted a seed. The seed was small, and its promise was buried deep within the relationship between God and humanity. With each generation of descendants, God brought the growth of this seed closer to the surface. The seed of Abraham quickly turned into the "Root of David." And eventually this Root sprung out of the ground through the manifestation of God's grace, Jesus Christ. Sin caused the Fall of humanity in the garden, separating us from the Tree of Life. God took a seed of His love and grace for His children, planted it with a person who would apply faith, and caused that little seed of grace to become the new, living tree of life, Jesus Christ. And now, we are part of His family tree. The grace we now live off of started out as a simple, small, unrecognizable seed.

> *...My grace is sufficient for you, for My strength is made perfect in weakness...* (2 Corinthians 12:9).

I love Strong's definition here of grace. The Greek word is *charis,*[2] and the translation is "unmerited favor, undeserved blessing, a free gift." Grace carries way more power than we often recognize. We are saved by grace, and it is a foundational principle of our beliefs. However, this knowledge can often make some of the power and life in grace fade into the background. Grace becomes way too familiar, and though the familiarity may not breed contempt (as the saying goes), the familiarity of grace can cause us to miss out on the depths of power and life that are within it and available for us to continue to live off of each day. Grace gives us life and life more abundantly, and then grace moves forward and multiplies through its recipients. Seeds always multiply.

Grace is packed full of life that never stops giving. It is a resource that multiplies forward without end. Grace has no lack because it comes from the storehouse within the Life Giver Himself. If we want life more abundantly, first we have to believe in it while it is only a seed. Then we must allow that small seed to become the foundation for our lives in Christ.

THE GRACE-SEED

The grace-seed is pregnant with abundant life. When faith is applied to such a seed, we begin to see the birthing of the multiplication and fruitfulness we are called to. Out of the seeds of grace, we see things happen we never would have dreamed possible when just looking at a seed. By all appearances, a seed is such a small and simple thing. A seed becoming a tree or a branch and bearing fruit seems like an impossible concept when we're looking only at the external appearance of this life-giving wonder. But when looking at that seed through faith (what could be inside) and planting it by that faith, we will see fruit that previously seemed impossible. We see how one seed, no matter how small or simple, can breed life and life more abundantly.

God as the Life Giver distributes the seeds. But we do not always get to see the life that is inside. In fact, we have missed out on the life in so many seeds given to us that a culture of doubt has been created within us. For a seed to be brought to life, be fruitful, and multiply, it must have faith applied to it; otherwise it remains only a seed. It only lives up to its external potential. The lack of life we see is not the fault of the seed or of the Life Giver, but it is due to our lack of faith in the Life Giver and what He gives. God always offers life. Everything He gives us has life hidden inside of it. But instead of breeding life, many times we just get worn out and overburdened by carrying around a growing sack of dormant seeds.

The Life Giver does not give burdens; He gives small, simple opportunities to see new life—and more life—spring forward. We must see everything the Lord has put before us as a seed and then apply active faith. His grace is constantly pregnant with new and abundant life, and He waits to birth the impossible out of every situation or circumstance. He waits for us. He waits for faith. The world will never know Him as the Life Giver or be able to embrace the seeds He has given us if we as the Body do not begin applying faith to every seed, circumstance, opportunity, or impossibility that He so generously gives us.

Naturally speaking, both a father and a mother are required to bring life to a baby. We as the Church are the Bride of Christ. If we do not face our Bridegroom with faith, we cannot prove Him as Life Giver. God has so much life to give, but if we do not receive the seed of His grace with faith, we cannot see life come forth. We must not be a barren bride married to One whose seed is so fertile and full of life! God has not given us grace just so we would receive the seed, but so that we would prove the fruitfulness and multiplication that's living within that seed. It is not because life has not been offered that we see so many with life being stolen from them. It is because we as the Bride are not always operating in the faith needed to prove the life the Father has offered.

There is abundant life waiting to spring forth from His grace, and it is available to the masses. This abundant life is available to the hurting, the barren, the needy, the dying, the poor, the sick, and the broken. And we are not just talking about eternal, abundant life, but about life more abundantly here on earth as it is in Heaven. The Life Giver is waiting for us to show the world that the life in His grace is not just for us, but that He's waiting for them, too. As a husband and wife come together, they do not do so just to enjoy life, but their purpose is very much to give life, to be fruitful and multiply. This is true physically and spiritually. In marriage *we* may know Him as the Life Giver, but through this multiplication, the *whole world* will know Him as the Life Giver.

THE SEED IN YOU

The "new" tree of life we are part of in Christ Jesus began with a seed of grace way back in the time of Abraham before the New Covenant of grace was ever established. Even though grace could not be seen yet, the seed planted with Abraham was the seed of grace. It was already full of life and was preparing to give life. The seed needed a fertile ground of faith to grow into the grace it has become. Instead of camping on our familiarity with grace, we must lean into this small, powerful seed frequently with the active power of faith. The pressure of faith brings to life all the abundant life that is hidden within the seed. This is the only way we will see the fullness of life God has for each of us. Imagine if Abraham's seed had fallen on faithless ground.

Right now you may have a lot of simple, small, unrecognizable seeds in your life. We can only dream about what each one possesses. One thing we do know: Each one contains some form of new and abundant life. There is a new tree of life in every seed! Abraham believed God, and his faith proved God as the Life Giver to generation after generation. The seed of grace in you is more than a gift from God or the right to be part of His family tree. The seed in you is grace enough to give life to a generation of sons and daughters who bear the image and likeness of the Life Giver Himself. What seeds of grace has the Life Giver deposited in your life? What could they grow and multiply into? Only faith will show.

HE HAS LIFE: IN HIS SPIRIT

Then He brought me back to the door of the temple; and there was water flowing from under the threshold of the temple toward the east, for the front of the temple faced east; the water was flowing from under the right side of the temple, south of the altar.

He brought me out by way of the north gate, and led me around on the outside to the outer gateway that faces east; and there was water, running out on the right side.

And when the man went out to the east with the line in his hand, he measured one thousand cubits, and he brought me through the waters; the water came up to my ankles.

Again he measured one thousand and brought me through the waters; the water came up to my knees. Again he measured one thousand and brought me through; the water came up to my waist.

Again he measured one thousand, and it was a river that I could not cross; for the water was too deep, water in which one must swim, a river that could not be crossed. He said to me, "Son of man, have you seen this?" Then he brought me and returned me to the bank of the river. When I returned, there, along the bank of the river, were very many trees on one side and the other.

Then he said to me: "This water flows toward the eastern region, goes down into the valley, and enters the sea. When it reaches the sea, its waters are healed. And it shall be that every living thing that moves, wherever the rivers go, will live. There will be a very great multitude of fish, because these waters go there; for they will be healed, and everything will live wherever the river goes" (Ezekiel 47:1-9).

This passage offers us so much hope in the Spirit of God! This river is often compared to the Spirit of God and the life He brings. God is taking us on a journey that often begins with ankle deep waters. Yes, the river and its living waters are powerful, but we need more than ankle deep. The Lord wants to take us farther, and He leads us out until we are knee deep in His Spirit and the life He offers. However, even knee deep is not nearly enough compared to what God has made available to us. We cannot stop at our knees and must not be content with less than God's best. The next part of the journey leads us into waist deep waters, a place we are often hesitant to go because then the life and pull of the Spirit has as much control over our lives as we do. It's a place of greater surrender, of letting go and trusting His current. The waters cover half our bodies, and letting go of our own currents, we are more subject to His pull. But still, even waist deep is nothing compared to the abundant life God is still calling us to. He wants to take us out another 1,000 cubits where the waters of His Spirit are so deep we cannot cross on our own. How often do we even think about going in a direction that is impossible on our own? We are caught up in the river of God, being led by the Spirit alone. We are swimming with the movement of God. Our own agendas are fading away, swept up in His love and power. And we are at the incredible mercy of the Spirit river of God.

Why would we want to go so far? Why would we want to let go and let God? Because wherever the Spirit river of God goes, it gives life! The waters flow out and are healed, as we saw in verse 9:

> And it shall be that every living thing that moves, wherever the rivers go, will live. There will be a very great multitude of fish, because these waters go there; for they will be healed, and everything will live wherever the river goes.

The Spirit of God gives life, multiplies life, and teaches us how to live new life! The abundant life we can partake of here on earth cannot be received or given out without surrendering full control and finding freedom in God's Spirit. The Spirit nourishes us in life-giving ways, soaking us in life and preparing us to give it out more abundantly. Everything lives! Can you imagine walking down a street where life has been stolen, killed, and destroyed in a broken or impoverished area? Then you realize that it is all waiting to be revived and transformed. All you need is to allow the Spirit river of God within you to overflow, because wherever it goes *everything lives!*

There will be fruit, there will be provision, and there will be a great catch of fish in our calling as fishers of people. That which was dying will have life. Those who are broken will be redeemed. Those who are sick will be healed. The blind will have sight, and the poor will overflow with abundance. We could go into these places and try to minister the best we can, and we may even see some fruit. But when the Spirit of God leads us, and when we take off our lid and let Him flow through us, the results are uncontainable. We don't have to try and build life; life just flows through us! The Spirit river of God is life more abundantly! In His Spirit there is freedom. This freedom releases new life to rise up, overflow, and give life to the desolate places. The Spirit river of God is flowing, and we must allow it to be a power in our paths. We must not fear the current, but only join Him. This is the overflow of the Life Giver and the Spirit who must flow through us to birth life.

There is a reason why major cities, towns, and villages were originally erected near rivers, lakes, and oceans. When planning for a city, you are planning for life. If you want to see life lived, you have to be near the water source that gives life to everything and everyone. The locations of large cities all across America, and all around the world, were chosen because of the water sources that offered life. People have created reservoirs and other life-giving sources, but they are just not the same as the real thing. Large populations of life spring up, live, and multiply all around the most powerful sources of water. What are we waiting for?

The Spirit of God within us wants to take our lives past the ankle deep waters, much farther than where the water rises to our knees or waist. That depth of water is not enough to give life to a new city or population. We have to trust God and go all in. The Spirit of the Life

Giver is a river inside of us full of life and everything that comes along with life. We do not have to direct it or control it, but we do have to remove our lid and let Him flow out.

This river of Life is ready to pour out of any of us who are open to overflow and multiply to a population and cause a new flourishing city of life to rise up. We cannot see this multiplication of life spring forth from our lives if we do not allow God to raise the standard of His Spirit in us. We must be a walking river where the waters bring healing, the trees are growing, the fruit is being born, and multitudes of fish are being caught. There is life waiting to be found in His Spirit, by His Spirit. In a life where we build many ponds for the thirsty to drink from, there is only one river that gives life wherever He flows. Are we leading others to a human-made pond, or are we being led by the river of God?

THE SPIRIT OF ADOPTION

For as many as are led by the Spirit of God, these are sons of God. For you did not receive the spirit of bondage again to fear, but you received the Spirit of adoption by whom we cry out, "Abba, Father" (Romans 8:14-15).

To have life in a city, you need a population. People carry out life. But to have people, you must have children—sons and daughters. God has so many children who still live like they are orphans. There are plenty of times when I have forgotten, and still forget, to live the life available to me as a child of the King. I bind myself in the law instead of living freely in His Spirit and grace. I put religious burdens upon myself that cloak me in a heaviness that is the opposite of life. I quench the Spirit river of God inside of me. How much it must pain God when I live in His house, but according to the rules of humanity or the former life I knew. An adopted child is not fatherless anymore, and he or she no longer lives in poverty. Adopted children take on the nature of the family they have been adopted into and all that comes with it. I have been adopted by God, and His Spirit made me born again and gave me new life. This new life must remain free and fresh each and every day.

As I mentioned in the Introduction, we experienced this with one of our adopted daughters. Regardless of the rest of the family and whether we were moving forward full of joy, communication, or laughter, she could not partake. She was living out the bondage of past and former prisons even while she was free. It broke our hearts watching the prison she was in. We cannot go forward in active faith if we are still in bondage to former fears. We have received the Spirit of adoption, and He gives new life. We must not accept this new, free gift like shameful servants still in bondage, but as those who are made new. Do you live each day like He has made you new? I know my life and the lives of people around me will be full of that much more of life when I allow myself every day to live outside old mindsets and in His newness.

We must live this new life according to the Spirit of adoption, who brings us into a Kingdom family where earthly impossibilities are made possible. Slavery is bondage, and God has not called us *slaves,* or even *servants,* anymore but *friends, family, sons,* and *daughters.*

The Spirit of God creates and validates the life of a son or daughter of God. When we are born again, the Spirit enters our lives, gives new life, and begins to shape and mold what our lives in Christ should look like. That is why we call this experience being "born again." I have been born, conceived anew with life that flows from the Spirit of God. The Spirit of adoption is the One who gives us life as His own, as well as all the heavenly rights, privileges, and authority that comes with being a son or daughter of God. We can now go into His house and live, not by past laws, but by faith according to His family freedom.

If you know your Father values loving and giving to the poor, He will only be pleased when you take what is His and declare it to them. If you know your Father feeds the multitudes, He will be a very proud Papa when you ask Him to multiply the seeds in your hands. The Spirit of adoption does not just save our lives, but He brings us into lives of co-laboring with our Father. I love when I see our kids take initiative based on what they see in our hearts. I love when they ask and give according to what is available. I love when they live in the fullness of the lives they have been given. And if I love that, how does our Father feel when we not only live, but freely give the life that the Spirit of adoption has given us? The thief tries to bring a counterfeit into every strategic move of God. If we are adopted by God and born anew, the thief will try to make us think or live like orphans, from a place of fear, shame, and helplessness. But when we are born again, each of us, every day, should declare with the prophet Micah, *"But truly I am full of power by the Spirit of the Lord"* (Micah 3:8). The Spirit has redeemed us from our orphan state (see John 14:18), so the enemy has nothing he can do except try to make us think according to our old lives rather than the Holy Spirit's new life that is already alive within us, wanting to come out in fuller form.

When we adopted our two older daughters, they immediately received our last name and all the rights that come with being part of our family. A great example of this would be their citizenship and right to enter the United States. Suddenly they transitioned from being limited travelers who must go through an intense and difficult process to receive entry into America and became citizens with free privilege to enter the country. Their rights and their authority changed. They have new life shaped not by the difficult circumstances they have come from, but by the present and future God has in front of them, which has actually been stamped on their passports. No longer are they characterized as "orphans," a name with a poor, needy, or shameful connotation. They entered a life without such a label, free to allow Christ to put His new mark upon them. They don't have to prove the last name on their new passports; they simply walk in the authority and life it brings them. Adoption gave them new life, and Destiny and I want them to partake of it to God's best. How much more life has the Spirit of adoption made available to us? Are we using our new heavenly privileges and passports? I would be crushed to see our daughters live their new lives within the bondage of how they grew up. I want them to be free to truly live the new lives they have been adopted into—lives of grace, freedom, and abundant life!

We are often fascinated (as we should be) by how God gave life while hovering over the earth at creation. We are in awe of Moses who glowed from meeting with Him face to face. God's grace has given life to us through the greatest gift ever, the life, death, and resurrection of Jesus Christ! But perhaps the greatest way God operates and reveals Himself as the Life Giver today is through His Spirit within His sons and daughters. The world will not know Him as the Life Giver He is unless we allow Him to be such in and through our lives. We forget what a miracle God has made of us. We are the creative workmanship of Christ, children of God, co-heirs with Christ Jesus. If we truly want to know Him and reveal Him as the Life Giver, we as His sons and daughters must simply take off our lids, receive from Him, and open our spouts. And as my daughter would sing the teapot song, "Tip me over and pour me out!" We know Him as the Life Giver, but the world is waiting for the Life Giver to be further revealed through us. A Father is revealed through His children.

ENDNOTES

1. Bill Johnson, *Face to Face with God* (Lake Mary, FL: Charisma House, 2007); iBethel Podcasts: "The Greater Glory," "Made for His Glory," "Transformed Series: From Glory to Glory"; www.ibethel.tv.

2. James Strong, *Strong's Exhaustive Concordance of the Bible,* Greek #5485.

Chapter 4

FULL
OF LIFE

NO one has ever given life without first being full of life. No mother has ever given birth without conceiving a child or carrying that child within her. Life must always begin in us before it can be given from us to those around us. The Father's love has come down and made its way into our lives. His love is the seed that causes us to be full of life and able to multiply. We must engage Him in the purity and simplicity of His love so that seed can have root in us before that seed is ready to multiply. Life is governed by love. As much as we are called to take that love and give life to others wherever we go, it must never, ever distract us from our First Love. He is where life begins.

I am a romantic at heart. When I first met my wife, I loved to woo and communicate with her in any way possible. I would drive 30 minutes before school just to put a rose on her car window. Sometimes I would stay up late and then wake up early to write and deliver a love letter that I could not get off my heart. That's probably why I love the "love letters" Jesus wrote to us in the Book of Revelation. Interestingly enough, these letters were communicated to the Church through John, who is uniquely referred to in Scripture as "the Beloved disciple."

These letters are some of my favorite parts of Scripture. They are very real, direct, and final messages from Jesus to His Beloved Bride. Some may look at these letters and shift in their seats over some of the rebukes involved. But God only chastens those He loves. For Him to remove John from society, take him all the way to the Isle of Patmos, and communicate so supernaturally, yet specifically, there had to be a lot of love involved. As we look at being full of life and ready to live and give life more abundantly, I can't take my eyes off of one of these revelatory letters. God is drawing His Bride to His side and preparing her to give life. But first He is wooing her back to Himself, to her First Love, so she can be full of life and ready to multiply.

THE LOVELESS CHURCH

To the angel of the church of Ephesus write, "These things says He who holds the seven stars in His right hand, who walks in the midst of the seven golden lampstands:

'I know your works, your labor, your patience, and that you cannot bear those who are evil. And you have tested those who say they are apostles and are not, and have found them liars; and you have persevered and have patience, and have labored for My name's sake and have not become weary.

'Nevertheless I have this against you, that you have left your first love.

'Remember therefore from where you have fallen; repent and do the first works, or else I will come to you quickly and remove your lampstand from its place—unless you repent.

'But this you have, that you hate the deeds of the Nico-laitians, which I also hate.

'He who has an ear, let him hear what the Spirit says to the churches. To him who overcomes I will give to eat from the tree of life, which is in the midst of the Paradise of God'" (Revelation 2:1-7).

Love,

Jesus

A dutiful but loveless Bride has no life to give. She cannot fulfill her calling without intimacy. Without being full of love, she cannot take care of the Father's children. Without love, she cannot herself be fruitful and multiply. It does not matter how ready she is to be a life-giving mom to the world and all God's children, she must renew the priority of her romance with Jesus. She has gifts inside of her that are created to give life, but they are dormant and awaiting her First Love's seed. She lives in a society where the family order has become so work-focused and need-focused that she thinks she hasn't any time for her Redeeming Love. Meanwhile, the Life Giver waits for her and life waits inside of her, and when the two meet there will be a revival of life inside and out. When she is full of life, she will become the Mother that God has called her to be, one that never forsakes her First Love or all His children around the world.

The loveless church had works, but no power behind her works. She was a mystery of potential that lacked God's potency. I could not love my kids more than I do, but I cannot let that love get in the way of romancing my bride. My wife and I need to have weekly dates, dream God-sized dreams together, and sometimes take a weekend getaway to be revived. How can I be a good life-giving parent to my kids each day if I do not operate from a place of life and joy myself?

For example, the kids in Ethiopia from the streets need to be kept warm from where their lack meets the cold, but the best and most lasting ways we impact their lives are fueled and powered by our own intimate exchanges with the Lord. A blanket will go a long way to keep the kids warm. But there is an even greater fire they can feel, a fire that spreads, when those in need come into live contact with God's fresh, intimate presence on our lives. I don't have the same life to inject if I don't keep my priorities straight. Even so, our love relationship with God goes far beyond our "priority"; He must remain our consuming passion! The world is waiting to be set ablaze, and Jesus Himself said He came to set the earth on fire. Our passionate, relentless pursuit of God Himself resembles two sticks rubbing closely together whose friction results in a spark and perhaps an uncontrollable flame!

If we will experience revival in the world, that revival must begin in us. If we will see the lost and broken restored to God's family, our family, we must begin with returning to our First Love. We must renew our romance of redemption where He picked us up, cleaned us off, and made us His own.

The thief has certainly been having his way. He has been stealing, killing, and destroying life around the world and even in our very own families at times. And most of all, he has been stealing our passion for our First Love. We are called to go and give life more abundantly back to all those people and places, just as Jesus did for us. Life will flow out of us, out of the wellsprings of our hearts. And just as Jesus promised at the end of His love letter, we will eat from the tree of life, with lots left over for the lost and broken. Like the 12 baskets of food leftover after feeding 5,000 from nothing (see Mark 8:19), God will take what we bring near to Him, speak to the rock inside of us, and gush out His rivers of living water. Many around the world are waiting for a good, healthy taste of life. What fruit and what water, for that matter, are we giving them? If we return to our First Love and once again become *one* with our Life Giver, then we will be life-givers *with* Jesus.

VACATION WITH GOD

I love to take time with the Lord. I am not just talking of a daily quiet time or devotions, but of real, full, and passionate times with God. Times full of praise, worship, prayer, refilling, and rumblings between my heart and His that I can't even describe. I suppose these times look different for us all during different seasons of our lives.

However, a vacation with God is different. I take time with my wife each day. We talk, we pray, we go outside and beyond our routines and daily cycles. But even our fresh times each day cannot take the place of those special memories when we have gotten away to a remote cabin, a cool and windy coastal area, or a gorgeous beach. Those memories are special and wonderful. This is not to say these vacations should be relied upon or replace our daily joys and interactions. Rather, they serve a unique purpose. Our vacations are for special memories, rest, relaxation, renewal, fun, laughter, and encounters with one another that can't be had in our own home or daily life. For these very reasons, we all need vacations with God.

We need to let down our burdens and lift them up into His hands. We need to escape our pressures and let God drape us with a Spirit-woven Hawaiian shirt. How effective would you be at life or your job if you never used your vacation time? How fresh would your marriage be without the occasional weekend getaway? Likewise, how can we expect to keep the fire of God in our lives if we don't mix it up with our First Love?

Think about this for a second. Honestly, how many lives have been conceived from an anniversary vacation? How many babies began their journey on a Valentine's getaway? This time away does not become the norm, but it is a great place to consistently rekindle that which God wants to set fire to.

God's priority is to give life through us to all those who need His love: those who are lost, broken, dry, and hurting. But we will never see that love come to life if we don't first allow God to deposit life in us. When we get away with God, we are privy to fresh encounters of life that can multiply for generations. When we set ourselves apart with Him, we find the root of the fruit He plans to bear from our lives. God has so much planned in and through our lives, but we shouldn't jump to the fruit of our future without embracing the power behind His romance.

MY FIRST LOVE!

As far as attire goes, I am normally a pretty casual guy. Dressing up for me usually consists of a button-up collared shirt—untucked, unbuttoned at the top, sleeves rolled up—and some khaki pants. I've just never been much of a tie kind of guy. I will wear a tie occasionally, and I might occasionally enjoy it when I do, but it's not very often.

I will never forget Valentine's Day 2010. I was speaking at our local church in Addis Ababa, Ethiopia. I had spoken there several times before, but it is an Amharic-speaking church (the local language), and I always had a translator when preaching. Thankfully, this church had one of the more well-known and extremely gifted translators from the area on staff, Pastor Menelik. He had translated for me several times before, and it always gave me comfort knowing that he was helping communicate the message.

Pastor Menelik knew me pretty well, so he knew my casual dress habits were likely in order. He had come to expect them. But this one particular Valentine's Day, I was speaking about returning to our First Love. As you may be able to see from this chapter, I am more than passionate about my First Love. I always want the Lord to know just how much I love Him, I always want to learn to love Him and know Him more, and I am jealous over knowing Him in such a way. It is of the utmost priority to me that God is always honored as my First Love. Because of this, I will often dress up a little more when preaching on this subject. My outward appearance does not affect my message in the slightest, but when it comes to my First Love, I want Him to feel extra special, just as I would dress up for a special date with my wife. Since this particular Sunday was Valentine's Day, what better day to honor my Jesus in such a way?

I was sitting in the front row during worship, while waiting for Pastor Menelik, my translator, to arrive. I was much more dressed up than usual: black slacks, black collared shirt that was tucked in, and a shiny pink tie in honor of Valentine's Day. I will always remember Pastor Menelik's face when he walked in the room. He took one glance at me and laughed out loud. After walking over to my side, he leaned in and whispered an explanation in my ear, "You know, Joey, I woke up this morning to get dressed, and as I reached for my suit and tie, I thought about it and remembered it was you who was speaking. I said to myself, 'I have never seen Joey in a necktie.' So I decided to be more casual myself. And here you are the first time I have seen you in a tie."

Pastor Menelik continued laughing, and I joined in as well. Most services, he probably would have been right. He could have assumed I would have shown up ready to go into God's presence, but very casually dressed. This Sunday, however, was different. It was Valentine's Day, and I was speaking about my First Love.

Just like in our marriages and relationships, it is often the little things that matter most and reflect our intentions. So, even knowing that my shirt and tie have zero effect on the words coming out of my heart and mouth, when I am talking about my First Love, I am more inclined to pull out all the stops, button all the buttons, and show up for our date with a tie on.

First Love is not just an important message to me; it is my number one priority in my personal life and something I am always trying to get better at. I went for years at one point in my life without ever allowing anything to sit on top of my Bible. Was I superstitious? No. I had no ill-conceived belief that it was detrimental in any way if something sat on top of my Bible. But even though it had no impact on anyone else, or any tangible impact on me or my Bible, this practice was always a reminder to me that I didn't want anything in my life to be set on top of my First Love. Though it made no direct impact in my spiritual life, it was one more thought that reminded me to stay hungry for Him each day.

Some messages, services, and conferences stick out when I look back on them, and some blend in to my memory. But there is one in particular I will never forget. I was speaking at an outdoor event in Southern California. Once again, the Lord had really burdened my heart for the "First Love" message. It was special to Him and special to me as well.

As I began to speak about my First Love, looking up and declaring that "it is all about Jesus" over and over again, a quiet power fell upon us and submersed us in God's presence. After the service, a dear friend and gifted intercessor approached me. I always appreciate the encouragement and prayers of those who are so gracious to share with me after I speak and am blessed whenever anyone takes that time. This time was extra special, as what this person said has always stuck out in my heart. This dear intercessor shared with me, "When you began to speak His name as your First Love, I literally saw and heard the Spirit come and whoosh over this whole place with a quiet 'Sshhhhhhhhhhh' because He was so honored and jealous over the love and intimacy being spoken of." Few compliments could mean more to me because if there is anything I want the Lord to be, it is loved, honored, and lifted up. The best kind of ministry starts with ministering to Him in this way. I want Him to feel special, and to imagine He was blessed in that way rattles me to my very core. I love my First Love, but I want to love Him more.

I put the utmost priority on living and walking with my First Love, and I am determined that I always will. I am committed to such.

But even with such a heightened focus on this essential part of God's and my relationship, I continually find that, much like the church at Ephesus, there is a height I must return to daily. I realize I have fallen when I find those moments—or perhaps those days, or regrettably even those weeks—when I have forsaken my First Love in even the smallest of ways. I must not permit myself to ever put any other part of my Christianity on top of my passion for His intimate presence.

I can try and disguise it without even recognizing what I have done. I can keep God high on the list, but high on the list does not matter if this kind of First Love intimacy and priority is not at the very top. He may still rule the roost in this way with my mouth, words, thoughts, and actions, but the true test comes back to my focus and my time. Have I been *showing* Jesus—more than just telling Him— that He is my First Love? Have I let Him drop even a notch from pursuing the high place His and my intimate relationship deserves? What height have I fallen from and where do I need to return? Or, should I perhaps grow so pro-actively desperate for Him that I rise before I fall? Return to your First Love!

THE DISCIPLE WHOM JESUS LOVED

Can you imagine, of all things, having this as your identity from the Lord? I cannot imagine a higher calling than to be identified by God Himself as one who shared such extraordinary intimacy and love with Christ. And the operative word here is *shared*. This is where our anointing and our fruitfulness come from. Jesus had a perfect and unconditional love for His disciples, friends, and followers, just as God does for all His children. However, what set John apart was that John shared that same unconditional, selfless, passionate, jealous love back with and toward Jesus. God's love and devotion is there for us all. Sharing requires something mutual. God's love extends toward all of us in such a "beloved" way. But not all of us offer that back. John did. John knew his First Love, pursued his First Love, and above all else, stayed true to his First Love.

Like an intimate friend one trusts, Jesus shared His deepest, longest-running secrets with John—end-time secrets we are still trying to unlock. Jesus could trust such to John because John was so jealous for God. He was jealous for His time, His affection, His words, and His glory. John was jealous for Jesus' love, and he so did not want the world to take one iota of that love away from Him that he spent his available time with Christ, laying his head upon His chest. I have and always will honor that moment that John and Jesus shared. How often I find myself in prayer, trying to draw close enough to God to lay my head upon His heart. John got His heartbeat, the very heartbeat of Life Himself. As we said about Moses' shining face: I want what he got!

Jesus had such a closeness with John that He whisked him away from everything and everyone else to an isle where nothing existed, a place where nothing could get in the way. God removed John from the world to a place where He could have him all to Himself. It was a place where Jesus could reveal Himself supernaturally to the man who would write the Book of Revelation about what the world would face ahead. Jesus could do so because he, John, was full of life, and he was calling others to be just as full. From a worldly point of view, being separated to this isle may have seemed like a punishment. But in reality, John just loved a jealous God. When we find ourselves in those desert isle times, we must remember that perhaps we're not being punished or sent to the wilderness; perhaps we are in the place where God's most revelatory, fresh fruit and life begin.

ENOCH

Enoch was known for very little in the Bible. In fact, Enoch is only spoken of a few times. However, what we do know of Enoch in those few descriptions is that Enoch must have been full of life!

Enoch was so full of life that he overflowed enough for his son, Methuselah, to live over 930 years, the longest in history. Enoch was so full of life that he was taken up and never tasted death. I know, it sounds like I'm making one of those "Chuck Norris is so strong, he…" kind of jokes. But really, that's how much life Enoch had in him. He would be the Chuck Norris joke of that day and age. Instead, we have but few references about him in the Bible. However, I like to believe in the old adage, "Quality is more important than quantity." Enoch's biblical story may not have the same quantity of Christian heroism as someone such as Moses or Paul. But Enoch's life and testimony is one that gushes the same quality that came forth from both those heroes of the faith.

> *By faith Enoch was taken away so that he did not see death, "and was not found, because God had taken him"; for before he was taken he had this testimony, that he pleased God* (Hebrews 11:5).

Now there is another testimony that I want: to please God. With as few mentions as there are of Enoch in the Bible, what we do know is that he did not taste death, he pleased God, his son Methuselah was the longest-living person ever recorded, and Enoch walked with God (see Gen. 5:24).

That's a pretty quality list from Enoch: to have the Bible say that you pleased God, to give life from your own genes to the longest living human ever, and to never see death, but be taken almost jealously by the Lord. However, as much as I honor, am encouraged by, and am even drawn to those testimonies, I find that I have learned the greatest amount by the most simple, yet intimately powerful statement of all Enoch's testimony: he "walked with God."

One of those few places in Scripture that mentions Enoch is in Genesis 5, starting in verse 17. What's funny is that this passage is actually a genealogy. Admittedly, I will sometimes skip over these parts of Scripture. I'm usually hunting for new truth and revelation rather than family lineage, and sometimes I need to be reminded that there is incredible power and life in the family lineage. There is something very powerful in the mantle and the anointing that is passed down from one generation to another. This is the kind of multiplication we are called to—physically and spiritually. Nevertheless, the genealogies do not normally catch my attention like this one does. There's something unique, even special, about its content and even the way it is written. Follow me for a second and we will look together at evidence of how especially full of life Enoch was, how much his life overflowed to the world and people around him, and why.

Chapter 5 of Genesis is all about the family of Adam—that's where this genealogy begins. The genealogy flows in a very uniform way, with rote descriptions of each new family or generation. For instance, verses 6-8 say:

> *Seth lived one hundred and five years, and begot Enosh. After he begot Enosh, Seth lived eight hundred and seven years, and had sons and daughters. So all the days of Seth were nine hundred and twelve years; and he died.*

And the same pattern is followed in verses 9-11.

> *Enosh lived ninety years, and begot Cainan. After he begot Cainan, Enosh lived eight hundred and fifteen years, and had sons and daughters. So all the days of Enosh were nine hundred and five years; and he died.*

In fact, each generation listed in the genealogy follows the same rote pattern describing the person's life. For each person it says that he "lived" however many years, and then it lists the name of his first-born son. The descriptions go on to say how many years the person lived after his first son was born, and then tell us that he had sons and daughters. Each description then lets us know how many years the person lived in total, only then does it simply say, "and he died."

What I find so interesting is that after following the same exact pattern all through this genealogy, we get to Enoch, and there is some sort of hiccup. For some reason, perhaps some special reason, Enoch doesn't fall into the same pattern as everyone else. This leads us to deduct and believe that Enoch didn't live an ordinary life, but was perhaps marked with life.

The genealogy's description of Enoch is given as follows:

> *Enoch lived sixty-five years, and begot Methuselah. After he begot Methuselah, Enoch walked with God three hundred years, and had sons and daughters. So all the days of Enoch were three hundred and sixty-five years. And Enoch walked with God; and he was not, for God took him* (Genesis 5:21-24).

The first part of Enoch's life is described just the same as everyone else's, stating how many years he lived before his first son was born. But after this, where every other person's description says how many more years they "lived," Enoch's says how many more years he "walked with God." Enoch did not just live; Enoch walked with God! There is a seemingly small, but *huge* difference. And we see the fruit of it in the description of Enoch's life. For at the end of Enoch's description it doesn't say, "and he died." Enoch's story tells us that God took him. Walking with God is such an intimate form of living life. In this life, we easily become what or whom we are beholding, without fail. Enoch walked so closely with the Life Giver Himself that Enoch became full of life. He was so full of life that he did not taste death. And before being taken up, these genes of "life" Enoch had received from the Life Giver overflowed into his son, Methuselah, who then had a greater quantity of life than any person before or since.

Enoch lived out an incredible testimony in the few lines of the Bible that discuss him. He never tasted death, his son lived longer than anyone else, and he had the straight-up incredible testimony of "pleasing" God. But none of these would have been possible if Enoch did not carry the testimony of one who did not just live, but who walked with God.

Being with my First Love does not always mean sitting quietly in a time of intimacy. Romantic dinners are not the only time my wife and I interact. Throughout the day, we talk, share moments together, put our thoughts together, go places together, love others together, and so much more. Being with our First Love is not just the daily devotions that we as believers start our day with, but the devotion, motives, focus, and intimacy we live according to. Intimacy with my wife is not just something that happens in private. She and I share intimacy while laughing at an inside joke, locking eyes from across the room, being in God's presence together, and so much more. God wants to share this same kind of real relationship with us.

As followers of Christ, our First Love intimacy with God is not just relegated to quiet, isolated prayer times, though I don't know what I would do without those. No, our First Love intimacy with God is a constant, life-living, life-giving connection from and through which all things flow. It is in the truest sense what John spoke of in John chapter 15 as "abiding." That's what Enoch did. That is what made Enoch so special. And that is why Enoch was so full and overflowing with life.

Walking together signals a number of things. It demonstrates relationship, symbolizes closeness, and reveals that two people are going the same direction. You can only walk *with* someone if you are going the same direction, at the same pace, toward the same goal or purpose. To me "walking with God" denotes perhaps the greatest kind of intimacy we could ever know with our First Love because it reveals not only union, but joint purpose and will. Enoch lived it out in an overflowing sort of way. If we will walk with the Life Giver Himself—not just sit with Him, but walk with Him in a life-giving kind of way—we will have more life in us in one moment than a large quantity of life could ever give.

LIVING AND GIVING FREELY WITH MY FIRST LOVE

All the things of self cause us only to "live" life. We become so busy pursuing all that we want to do, all that we need, all that is required of us by the world. But even if we achieve it all, don't we just end up like the others in the genealogy with descriptions of how many years we lived, who our kids are, and when we died? I don't know about you, but I want more than that. I want to be full of life! I want to share that "Beloved" kind of relationship with Jesus like John had. I want to "walk with God" like Enoch did. I want my life to ooze and overflow more life. When all is said and done, will you blend into that same genealogy? Or will you share a similar hiccup with Enoch as someone who did not just live life, but who was full and overflowing with Life Himself?

For me, while still in this world, there is perhaps no greater definition to living "life more abundantly" than to be living freely and giving freely with my First Love. That is when I know that I am full of life!

Chapter 5

OFFENSE VS. DEFENSE

WHEN it comes to professional sports, and especially in regard to the NFL, one will often hear or speak the phrase, "Defense wins championships." It's part of an ongoing debate, sort of in keeping with the "Which came first, the chicken or the egg?" argument. The argument leaves one deciding whether a stout defense or a dynamic offense is more likely to produce a championship.

It's easy to be swayed by offense. Offensive players are the smoking guns, the high-octane attack always geared to score points and entertain the fans. This is often the natural draw of the casual fan. But because of the frequent draw to offense, we hear these phrases thrown about quite a bit, "Offense sells tickets," but "Defense wins championships." It is the argument that offense may score points and drive fans crazy with excitement, but when it comes down to winning, it is a good defense that wins championships. Defense has been at the foundation of a lot of great teams, dynasties even, and a lot of memorable victories.

Sometimes I wonder if we as believers have subscribed to this belief. My question is: have we as believers gone on the defensive? Offense and defense are two entirely different mindsets. Both are absolutely necessary to remain standing and achieve victory. But I wonder whether "offense vs. defense" should even be a debate as followers of Christ. Oftentimes, it isn't a debate at all, especially in the American Church. We have clearly fallen into a pattern of defense. This might be OK if we were going after championships, but not when we are applying Christ's victory to giving life, loving others, and redeeming family. God has called us to live our lives on offense. Jesus has assured us the victory through the cross and His resurrection. Countless times throughout Scripture, God has promised to be our defense, our protector, and to never to leave us or forsake us. This leaves us with an offensive calling and absolutely nothing to fear.

We are called to offense to further establish the victory of Christ for the world. Is it possible then that we spend too much of our time living defensively based lives? Truly, in the life of the believer, the offense vs. defense debate comes down to love vs. fear. Which one do we live by? This is not to ask which one we believe in and want to live by. I don't believe any follower of Christ would readily come right out and say, "I live by fear." We know what we are supposed to live by. But the true question is: Which of these is the true motive behind our daily decisions and actions? Then we must decide: How do we cross over?

WALKING THE STREETS: OFFENSE OR DEFENSE?

One of the foundation points of our mission and family in Ethiopia was walking the streets according to John 10:10.

> *The thief does not come except to steal, and to kill, and to destroy. I have come that they may have life, and that they may have it more abundantly.*

The whole base of the movement going forward in Ethiopia began with us learning to live with an offensive mentality on the streets— wherever we went and whomever we were with. We did not have a vehicle during our time in Ethiopia, so we were very reliant on public transportation and spent a good bit of our time walking all across the city. As much as this could be an inconvenience, it was a blessing in disguise. It kept us with the people. Walking the streets built relationships; it taught us the culture in a very raw form. Destiny was pregnant with our second biological daughter, Galilee, when we first moved there. This was quite a sight: Destiny, Mercy, and me walking the streets, blonde-haired and blue-eyed, a pregnant belly protruding from Destiny, endlessly walking and trying to love and give life like Jesus would. You could say we stood out just a little bit. In fact, you may have laughed had you seen us.

This was not always easy, but it was always worth it. This drew a lot of attention at times, which sometimes could be used as a platform to show Christ's love, and at other times it drew very unwanted attention full of threats, criticism, and the like. As we woke up to approach the streets each day, we had a choice: offense or defense? The enemy would try to attack our thoughts. He would try to frighten us from feeling safe to freely walk or freely distribute life through love. The enemy used his fear tactics to try and bully through our thoughts; he did not want us to play offense. And on those days, we had to really battle not to be swayed back to a fearful, defensive mentality.

I remember one day in particular that was quite the battle, but also quite a victory. I woke up that morning with a clear mandate from the Lord to go out on the streets with Alex and just walk. Alex grew up on the streets and knew them well, but was now living with us. God had something He wanted to do on the streets that day—or perhaps something He wanted to do in us. However, we had no money. We had 7 birr, which at the time was the equivalent of 50 cents, to support our family, who at the time included about ten people living in the house. Our power was out that day due to the power ration that frequently takes place, and our propane tank for our stove was empty. The enemy was trying to set us up, but God wanted us to go!

We needed funds not only for the family, but for a number of the street kids we were taking care of. God reminded us not to look at the circumstances, but to go out and give life according to what was in His heart rather than what was in our hands. I was just about to leave when Destiny suddenly got incredibly sick. I had not seen her in such pain for a long time. My first thought was whether or not I should stay home. Nope, I couldn't fall into the temptation to play defense. God told me to go out and play offense. So, I went to Destiny and laid hands on her while praying. She agreed with me in faith, looking only to the Lord, and quickly felt better. Praise God!

I was just about to walk out the door when a quick need popped up. Our toilets were not flushing due to some of the issues with water and plumbing, so we were flushing our toilets with buckets. This is a very common thing. My family needed me to fill the bucket before leaving because it was too heavy for them to lift on their own. I went to fill the bucket, and while leaning over, my back suddenly went out. I could not remember the last time my back had gone out. It felt like a crack had just spread up and down my spine. It was some of the worst pain I could remember in a long time. Again, the enemy was trying to keep us from offense.

As I lay on a special ball we have for stretching, now with Destiny praying over me, I inquired of the Lord as to what I was supposed to do. The Spirit spoke to my heart, "When you walk out that gate, your back will be completely healed." Well, that was that as far as I could see. It was time to go.

Just before leaving, still wincing in pain, I grabbed my ATM card. Our account was empty, but I felt prompted by the Lord to take it with me just in case something might come through. Alex and I approached our gate, sought the Lord as usual so as to ask Him to lead us, and then stepped out to walk with the Lord and give life to those who were hurting, broken, or begging on the streets.

About a block after leaving our house, I realized that all my back pain was now gone. By the grace of God, I had left it at the gate. Alex and I couldn't get a bus after waiting at our stop, so we continued on foot. Sometimes that was best anyway; it provided more opportunities to pray over people and ask God how to join Him. I learned a lot as we walked.

We had a couple of errands to run in the process, so we headed toward the direction they were in. Just to walk the streets and smile His light toward someone was opportunity enough on most days. But sometimes God had something more. This particular day we were close to where our stops were and were passing a row of shoe shiners, a trade that is very common among the streets and even more common among kids who live on the streets.

We walked past a long row of shoe shiners, and the Lord caught my attention. I saw a light over this young man, but due to our own fleshly agenda, we kept walking. The Spirit was nudging me to get my shoes shined. But there was a problem: I didn't want my shoes shined. I was wearing trail shoes that really did not need to be shined. But the Lord would not give up. Maybe it wasn't my shoes that needed shining; perhaps it was me and/or this man. The Spirit was convicting my heart over and again to go back and meet him. Finally, I obliged. I told Alex that there was someone back behind us God wanted us to meet and that I needed to get my shoes shined.

As he began to shine my shoes, we began to talk. Much of our conversation was through Alex's interpretation. The shoe shiner's name was Abraham. He came to the city from down country looking for work. He came from a Christian background, but was away from family and support. Just as he finished shining my shoes, I asked if we could pray over him. He nodded, so we laid our hands upon him and began to bless and call forth God's purposes in him. We blessed him to be who God had called him to be, to arise and shine with the life God had within his heart. It was a time to give life simply by reminding him of the Lord's love for him and calling forth God's purposes within him. It was a very simple time, but clearly God-ordained.

As I stood up to leave just after saying goodbye, I sensed the Lord speaking to my heart again. This time, the directive was quite different. God was directing me to the ATM. I reasoned that there was zero dollars in our account, and the ATM does not spit out money if there is zero money in there. However, I knew this was from God. We reached the ATM building, and I walked up according to what God had spoken. Then I asked the Lord how much I should take out. "The maximum amount," He said, which was 4,000 birr or about $250. I put in my card, entered my pin, and voila! Out came 4,000 birr without any hesitation or question. I was a little stunned. The money was not in the account. This ATM had never allowed money to come out that was not in there. I even knew its usual message by heart. But this day, that message did not appear. Jehovah Jireh appeared!

We now had the full provision we needed to take care of the street kids that night. Praise God! We also had enough money to get food for our home and our family as well as purchase a new propane tank. Thanks again, God!

The enemy clearly did not want us to go on offense that day. But every time we put our hearts back on offense and giving life, God showed up. Living from a mentality of defense can sneak up on us. The thief just feeds us one reasonable circumstance after another until he can get us to agree with his deterrent. Sometimes God will give us wisdom to pause, wait, or not take a particular step. But this should come from God, not fear or circumstance. We have to fight through our circumstances and stay on offense. As I said before, we had to battle in a variety of ways many times while walking the streets of

Addis Ababa. Each time, we had a choice to make: offense or defense? Survive life or give life? We did not always choose correctly, but every time we did we saw God show up.

You have a choice each and every day. What faith or mentality are you living from when you get up in the morning? How do you see people, circumstances, or the world around you when you walk out your front door? What choice are you living out each day? Are you giving life or surviving it? To help strengthen this decision, let's look at some of the factors behind our two choices.

Because of the fact that Christ has clearly called us and set us up for offense, let's look first at defense. We want to address the defensiveness we've allowed to sneak into our lives. We need to look at it, identify it, focus on what God has called us to ahead, and move forward once and for all in an offensive strategy that gives life to those who need it most.

DEFENSE

Offense vs. defense is the mindset, or faith, by which we live our lives. It is a motive by which we make our decisions and invest our time, resources, thoughts, and actions. Defense comes from a mindset of protection. It is something we do to safeguard that which is important to us. We protect our lives, our families, our reputation, our belongings, and much more. Essentially, defense is the method we use to solidify our security, whether it be financial, physical, or the like. I am not speaking of defensive mindsets in this way to try and say we should be careless. But we often use wisdom solely for the sake of defending what we have instead of applying it as part of our offensive strategy to move forward, advance, and multiply. The Bible calls us to be wise as serpents but as peaceful as doves (see Matt. 10:16). To us, this should mean that we are wise to the enemy's tactics, remaining aware so as not to be lured in to his lies. But it also means that we should be so aware of God's promises of care, love, protection, and victory that we can stand firm and move forward in life while remaining as peaceful as doves, even in circumstances that contain no peace whatsoever. If anything, this verse gives us even more assurance of the fact that we can go on offense without worry of loss. God's got our back, and we must peacefully trust that to be true.

Defensive strategy is something used to stop the opposition from scoring. It is designed to hold our position, prevent the opposition's gain, and keep us from experiencing loss. But, I have never seen defense win anything unless it suddenly changes gears and goes on the offensive. By itself, defense truly becomes a futile effort of self. It is unnecessary unless being used in balance and as a strategic way to reinforce the power and direction of our offense. This point grows even larger when we have received the promise from God Himself to defend and protect us. When we live according to defense, our actions are essentially telling God that we do not trust Him and that because of this lack of trust we must do His job for Him. Ouch!

What happens is we fear not keeping up with the world. We fear not having enough. We fear death. We fear what other people might think, which to some of us is worse than death. We fear the difficult experiences that our parents or their parents were plagued by. We fear the "what if's" of life. But I would venture to say that the "what if's" whispered into our ears each day are the offensive lies of the enemy, a predator who doesn't have teeth anymore. That enemy is relegated to inflicting deceptive thoughts of what he would do, might do, or could do if we weren't actually surrounded by the perfect, impenetrable love of God. The "what if's" of life are the enemy's strategy, lies, and imaginary threats that we often allow to dictate our direction and alter our call from those who are taking more ground to those who are protecting our current ground. When I realize the ways I have done or still do this, that's an even bigger ouch!

"PLAYING" DEFENSE

What is your strategy when you play freeze tag? I grew up playing it often when I was a kid, but I cannot remember what my strategy was then. However, I know what my strategy would be now! We discussed this briefly in Chapter 2, but I want to take another look at it to help reveal the battle we are in.

Freeze tag is another one of those games where we have a choice, a strategy if you will. We can choose to play it offensively or defensively. I won't repeat the rules of the game here, having done so in Chapter 2 and realizing that you very well may have played this childhood game many times.

When playing freeze tag, the number of those who are free far outweighs those who are "it" and looking to freeze the participants. Those who are "free" have the authority to give life, while the person who is "it" and tagging people only has the power to freeze someone momentarily, or until someone with an offensive mindset comes and sets the frozen one free.

When we play this game, we have to make a choice. Will we play defensively, protecting self with the number one goal of avoiding the freeze? Or will we play offensively, with our highest priority focused on victory for the entire team of those who are not the tagger? Freeze tag is such a perfect illustration of our choice as believers: we can give life on offense or fearfully protect our own life on defense. In freeze tag, offense vs. defense is a question of priority. Do we place a higher priority on temporal self-preservation or on overall victory with no one remaining frozen? Love wins! But we must allow that love to flow freely through us on offense.

I have allowed the enemy to cause me to look at or protect self far too many times. I am sick of the loss my self-preservation has most definitely caused, although often unknowingly. Any time, resource, or focus I place upon protecting or preserving self is a resource that could have been spent on giving life to others. This is not to say we are not to sustain our own life or family or even to enjoy some of the pleasure the Lord makes available to us. These choices are not defense; they are life. What it does mean is that we need to look at our measure and our motives if we are not freely moving forward and giving life on offense.

As believers, we are each a new creation. The lies and fears of the past have been exposed and destroyed. We cannot allow these old deceptions to put a limit on our new potential. These things keep us from walking by faith. They often sneak up without us recognizing them and masquerade as normal or acceptable parts of life. However, just because protecting self in some way has become culturally normal does not mean that we are abiding by a beneficial type of culture. Our culture often justifies our weaknesses. But God's Kingdom culture is defined by a love so perfect it squashes culturally acceptable old mindsets and redeems us from the roots up to live offensively powered lives that are fueled and invigorated by love. We all have one kind of fuel or the other: fear or love. The kind of fuel we are powered by in our decisions and our indecisions helps us realize if we are living life on defense or on offense.

THE OTHER RELATIVE

Previously, in Chapter 2, we discussed the story involving Ruth, Boaz, and "the other relative." The "other relative" and the decision he made is a perfect picture of a defensive mindset. This other relative is so often overlooked in this story, but his subtle example is one we must heed in our own lives. We must remain aware of this tendency to self-protect while we make what often look like the little decisions of life and turn them into a larger defensive mindset.

As we talked about in Chapter 2, Boaz was part of giving life to the nations. He and Ruth had their son, Obed. Obed and his wife had a child, Jesse. And Jesse gave life to David, who became the ancestor of Christ. Boaz's offensive mindset gave life and sparked such a multiplication that, through Christ, Boaz's offensive step toward Ruth changed the world. But before Boaz took this step of faith, Ruth was first obligated to the "other relative," who might have been a part of a similar offensive redemption. That is what happens often when we play defense in life: We miss out on God's blessing and His increase. The "other relative" may have been an incredible person. He may have been very godly and may have lived what many of us would consider an exemplary life. But in Ruth, this "other relative" was presented with a decision to make: offense or defense? Or perhaps even: faith or security? Let's look again at what Boaz said to Ruth and the close relative's response to Boaz:

> *Now it is true that I am a close relative; however, there is a relative closer than I. Stay this night, and in the morning it shall be that if he will perform the duty of a close relative for you—good; let him do it. But if he does not want to perform the duty for you, then I will perform the duty for you, as the Lord lives...* (Ruth 3:12-13).

> *And the close relative said, "I cannot redeem it for myself, lest I ruin my own inheritance. You redeem my right of redemption for yourself, for I cannot redeem it"* (Ruth 4:6).

Some of the wording in the above verse is interesting to me. First, the "other relative" was quoted as saying, *"I cannot redeem it for myself, lest I ruin my own inheritance."* Then he was again quoted as saying, *"I cannot redeem it."* I want to look closer at the word *cannot* in each statement. I am curious whether or not this "other relative" truly *could not* redeem Ruth, or if he was simply deceived by self into believing he could not because his eyes were on what he might lose rather than the life God might gain. Perhaps it was not that the other relative *could not* redeem Ruth; maybe the reality was that he looked at the parts of self that were at stake and he *would not* risk what could get caught in an offensive step of faith to give life to another. Risk is what keeps us from giving life on offense with God. Some steps are simply risk and shouldn't be taken. However, when God is in something, our step of faith is actually a step of obedience, and there is no true risk involved.

I am not in any way condemning this other relative. Actually, I am looking at my own life and asking the Lord about the things I have said I could not do, when in reality I was protecting self, and the truth of the matter was that I was unwilling to value giving life to others over temporal loss in my own.

I am so thankful that Boaz did not consider what might be lost in his redemption of Ruth. I want to be more like Boaz in this season ahead, and I pray God will raise up this Boaz anointing among us, among our neighborhoods, and among the nations. May we all step forward out of our defensive stances, redeem the Ruth's of our generation, live beyond the laws of humanity, and watch God give life to a redeemed generation that will change the world. I choose life! I choose offense!

OFFENSE

There is no fear in love; but perfect love casts out fear, because fear involves torment. But he who fears has not been made perfect in love (1 John 4:18).

This is where our offense starts—from His perfect love. Offense is possible because perfect love prevails. If we were not guarded by the perfect, impenetrable love of God, then we would probably have a lot more to worry about and offense by faith would be a lot more difficult. But since God has our back—as well as our front and all sides, for that matter—we can focus on offense. However, even when we know this in our thoughts, it has to make it down to our hearts. For this to happen, we must gain a new, more whole understanding of what His perfect love is. Without such, we may want to play offense, and we may even try to do so, but we will live in a state of timidity, hesitancy, and defensiveness. And that just will not do. A tentative, fearful offense can actually be more of a liability than a threat to take hold of victory. We must go all in.

The best offense originates from the true understanding of how perfect and impenetrable God's love for us really is. This is our foundation. Once we have this foundation firmly in place and supporting all our thoughts and actions, we can then move forward with an offensive advance that will take ground back from the thief, possess new land, and advance His Kingdom here on earth as it is in Heaven.

While living in Ethiopia, I had a few favorite sayings in the primary local language of Amharic. One of them was straight from this foundation. I said it loud, and I said it often. I spoke it to the poor on the streets, and I declared it over our local leadership team. "Egziahbir fikur fitsum neow!" (Egg-Zah-bih-here fick-ur fit-soom ny-oh.) God's love is perfect!

The problem is, when I say this out loud or to myself, I realize that my earthly comprehension of what is "perfect" is pretty lacking. Perfect in my eyes carries an earthly connotation. Basically, my idea of perfect is jaded by the imperfections of the world. But when God says His love is perfect, it is a supernatural perfection. I often think of it as a sphere around me with no gaps. It is impenetrable. There is no way that anything can touch me that doesn't go through God first, unless I welcome it through my own choices and agreements. As we move forward *with* God, His love perfectly protects us so that we can focus on the calling set before us—to give life! This is the kind of defense God plays on our behalf. Is there any possibility of losing if your defense is perfect? Is there any risk or chance of loss if the other team's attack is rendered ineffective? God's love is perfect, whole, without gaps, impenetrable. This removes any need to hold onto fear, and it takes with it any natural compulsion to play defense. This does not mean our earthly circumstances will always feel good from an earthly perspective, but it does mean we can trust that God is with us and that He has overcome the world because His love is perfect. If we realize how perfect God's love for us is, only then do we have the perfect defense.

If you are wholly confident in God's perfect, impenetrable love for you, then nothing will stop you from giving life to everyone around you from all He has made accessible to you. If you truly want to live your life on offense, ask God to give you an impenetrable faith toward His impenetrable love. We might not be perfect. Those around us are not perfect either, and neither is the world. But God's love makes up for all of that. It fills in every gap and surrounds us to such an extent that we can give our lives to the offense Jesus modeled, the offense He has called us to join Him in as givers of life. *"...I have come that they may have life, and that they may have it more abundantly"* (John 10:10).

This is exactly what Jesus was saying: He came to finalize our defense against the thief, but at the same time, He came to teach us to play offense, to commission us to do so, and to empower us by His Spirit to live it out! Jesus is saying that He sees the hurting places in our lives that have caused us to live defensively. He sees our empty places and our dry crevices. He came to give life back to each of those places. But He didn't stop there. Jesus knew God had His back, and He knew that God's promises were to impart life *more* abundantly. Jesus wouldn't just restore old land to our lives; He would take new ground, new land, and infuse that land with the promised land of Heaven. This is what we are called to do—advance the Kingdom and take new ground.

TAKING NEW GROUND

Let's take a look at a couple of people in Scripture who were both igniters of new moves of God. After the Fall of humanity, God turned to Noah to help save creation. But after all was stable, the Lord turned to Abram, or Abraham, as he was later known. There is so much in Scripture about Abraham to dive into and soak up. But for this purpose, let's look specifically at Abraham's obedience on Mount Moriah and God's blessing of life that followed after. This is, and probably always will be, one of those favorite passages of mine, the kind you find yourself back in year after year. Abraham left behind an incredibly special testimony and some pretty phenomenal promises from God.

> *Now it came to pass after these things that God tested Abraham, and said to him, "Abraham!" And he said, "Here I am." Then He said, "Take now your son, your only son Isaac, whom you love, and go to the land of Moriah, and offer him there as a burnt offering on one of the mountains of which I shall tell you"* (Genesis 22:1-2).

Abraham had already left all to follow God. He had believed God at His word with far less than we have today. And God had accounted it to him for righteousness. Then, just when it seemed that Abraham's promised land had come to fruition, God tested and strengthened Abraham yet again.

The promise of Isaac had come forward in Abraham and Sarah's life—an impossible promise nevertheless. And now, God challenged Abraham's heart by asking him to give it back, surrender, and trust Him with such blind faith in God's perfect love that he would put his son, his answered promise, on the altar.

Then on the third day Abraham lifted his eyes and saw the place afar off. And Abraham said to his young men, "Stay here with the donkey; the lad and I will go yonder and worship, and we will come back to you." So Abraham took the wood of the burnt offering and laid it on Isaac his son; and he took the fire in his hand, and a knife, and the two of them went together (Genesis 22:4-6).

This was a strategic moment for Abraham and creation as a whole. When God begins something new, He is going to see it all the way through, far beyond what we can see in that moment. God knew He could use Abraham to restart His offensive move and rebirth His family on earth, but He wouldn't allow Abraham into that position as a life-giver without knowing Abraham would not, could not, be moved. Not even by a lifelong dream or promise.

And Abraham stretched out his hand and took the knife to slay his son (Genesis 22:10).

That one still gets me. Do we always realize that God the Father actually went through with this kind of love on our behalf? In Abraham's story, most of us know that God provides before we even begin the story. But God actually stretched out His hand toward His own Son on our behalf. Wow! A little off subject, but it still blows me away.

Abraham trusted in God's perfect, impenetrable love so much that he did not even feel the need to play defense when his own son actually *was* on the verge of being lost. Abraham was so focused on the offensive assignment God had called him to that he could see beyond loss and prophetically grasp the victory of God.

Our youngest daughter, Galilee, has the middle name of *Moriah*. It has always been a special name to me because I believe Moriah is a place where multiplication of life begins. Moriah is the place where we are just starting to taste God's promise and the Lord gives us the option of doing us one better. He gives us an offer of obedience. He asks us to trust Him enough not to need to protect His promise. He asks us to entrust it back to Him knowing His perfect love for us removes the risk of loss and guarantees greater gain and multiplication. He challenges our motives to purify us. Are we in it for us or for Him? On Moriah, God is asking us what is in our hearts and what or who we are truly seeking. All the while, God has the love of an all-knowing Father. Behind His back, He has the promise in hand, tenfold! That's the kind of abundant Father we are loved by. After all, that is our milk-and-honey God!

> But the Angel of the Lord called to him from heaven and said, "Abraham, Abraham!" So he said, "Here I am." And He said, "Do not lay your hand on the lad, or do anything to him; for now I know that you fear God, since you have not withheld your son, your only son, from Me."
>
> Then Abraham lifted his eyes and looked, and there behind him was a ram caught in a thicket by its horns. So Abraham went and took the ram, and offered it up for a burnt offering instead of his son. And Abraham called the name of the place, The-Lord-Will-Provide; as it is said to this day, "In the Mount of the Lord it shall be provided" (Genesis 22:11-14).

I can remember several Mount Moriah moments in my family and my life. To be honest, I think we might be in the middle of one as I write this chapter. But hopefully that won't be true anymore by the time you are reading this. Because if it is, please pray for us!

These Mount Moriah seasons have been excruciating to be sure, but they were and are also amazing! It is where God asks us to join Abraham in walking up the mountain with our promise in hand. It is where God checks our peace and the trust in Him which births that peace. It is where we can make it to the top with love-filled tears in our eyes because we count it all loss compared to the greatness of knowing Him. *Moriah is where multiplication begins.* It is where a promise can go from one promise that blesses me, or perhaps my family, to a promise that is multiplied to bless a community, a nation, a generation, or more. Moriah was a strategic part of this new offensive move of God. And God often brings a Moriah in our lives when we are about to walk in the same. It can hurt, but we can just feel the Lord doing His thing inside us and all around us in the midst of it. Because truly, God wants to give us *more* than the promise! We cannot receive all He wants to give us until He strengthens us to hold onto what He wills to give. We let go of life, without evidence, simply because we trust that God truly is an abundant-life God.

The fact that Abraham followed God up Moriah with precious Isaac in hand blessed God enough to save Isaac and multiply the promise of Issac's life into an offensive strategy and a move of God that rocked the world. Abraham's obedient surrender and undying offensive faith became a vessel for God to restore to the world the life that was lost in the Garden of Eden and to give it back *more* abundantly!

> *Then the Angel of the Lord called to Abraham a second time out of heaven, and said: "By Myself I have sworn, says the Lord, because you have not withheld your son, your only son—blessing I will bless you, and multiplying I will multiply your descendants as the stars of the heaven and as the sand which is on the seashore; and your descendants shall possess the gate of their enemies"* (Genesis 22:15-17).

Every time I read through this passage I have one of those moments where I just want to stand to my feet and yell out, "Go God!" My wife usually rocks those shouts pretty well! Two powerful things happened in God's blessing of this new, offensive move. First, He promised multiplication—more multiplication than what was originally promised. Then God took the milk and honey a step further—a little *more* abundantly—and gave us a serious offensive statement that would be true for more than Abraham and his family. This offensive guarantee would be true for all those multiplying descendants who were just promised: *"...And your descendants shall possess the gate of their enemies."*

God calls Abraham to a tough obedience at the beginning of their relationship, and Abraham says yes. God follows up Abraham's obedience with a pretty amazing promise of a child to a barren couple. Then, Abraham continues on offense to such a level that he perseveres for years and years for that promise to come true. Just when that enduring promise has finally arrived, God strengthens Abraham's offensive focus once more on Moriah, and again Abraham says yes. God takes the promise He gave Abraham and turns it into countless promises. Then the Father takes this enduring father in Abraham and basically says, "Because you have not been about protecting yourself or defending what is rightfully yours, because you have remained focused on *My* offensive goals, I AM going to take every one of those multiplied promises and use every one of them for offense. And every one will take new ground for My Kingdom and possess the gate of their enemies." God took Abraham's commitment to offense and turned that offensive focus into an entire army of enduring saints who would advance Kingdom ground.

One of the biggest offensive keys in this story, outside of Abraham's focus on God alone, was in that last promise He made to Abraham: *"...And your descendants shall possess the gate of their enemies."* Sometimes I think we read or listen to this statement, hear the word *enemies,* and automatically assume internally that it means that our enemies won't prevail against us. And while that is true in our relationship with God, this promise is really saying that we (the descendants of Abraham) will move forward, stay on offense, and continue to take new ground as we maintain this offense, until our enemies' gate will not, and cannot, prevail against us. It is a promise of the new ground to be taken. We are called to offense because there is enemy territory in lives, families, communities, and nations that is waiting to be taken for the Lord. The ground guarded by the enemy is promised to us as Kingdom ground. But, we cannot take all the ground that has been promised unless, like Abraham, we are willing to obey, endure, and consistently push forward on offense. If we do, we will take new ground, and the promises of God in our lives will multiply new life of their own. Now *that* is a promise!

MORE OFFENSE, MORE NEW GROUND

Peter experienced something very similar in the New Covenant while following Christ. Abraham's offensive dedication paved the way for a new move of God that eventually brought forth Christ. Jesus came to begin a new offensive move the Father had been planning all along, and He came with the same powerful promises that had been given to Abraham.

Jesus was sitting with His disciples at Caesarea Philippi. He went through a very storied question and discussion time with them, specifically with Peter. This is when Peter declared that he knew Jesus was the Christ, Son of the Living God. Jesus followed Peter's answer with an incredible blessing. He gave him the keys of the Kingdom of Heaven, which is authority to bind and to loose on earth as it is in Heaven.

But there is one part of Jesus' revolutionary response and blessing over Peter that reminds us of what God promised Abraham. He gave an offensive promise that gives us further guarantee of new ground waiting to be taken. Jesus said, "*...On this rock I will build My church, and the gates of Hades shall not prevail against it*" (Matt. 16:18).

You don't get to someone else's gates unless you are on offense. That is what Jesus was saying. If—or perhaps better yet *when*—you go on offense and bang on the gates of the enemy, you will prevail and take that ground.

Just as God had done with Abraham in starting a new move of life, Jesus was now doing with Peter and His disciples. In both situations, with Abraham and with Peter, God gave the same promise: Neither the gates nor the land of the enemy will be able to stand up to the offensive onslaught of the life I will bring through you. God is doing everything possible to take His people's eyes off of what they need to protect by putting their eyes on what is within their reach. The promise is there to be taken!

We are called to go on offense with Jesus. The thief has been stealing hope, killing dreams, and destroying the family of God for far too long. We have seen so much of this that it can be very tempting to pull back and guard what we have left. But God sees the areas where the thief has stolen from people's lives and families. He sees the territory the enemy has surrounded with gates and bondages. The territory that was lost is waiting to be found. If we will go on offense, the things the thief has stolen and destroyed are promised to be ours. We can give life back to those places in people's lives, and we can give it back more abundantly because of He who lives in us. There is old land to be recovered, new territory to be taken, and abundant life to be given.

I am still learning how to consistently live my life on offense and to take all the new ground with God that I can. But I am committed to living and giving life on offense. Will you join me? Consider this our Mount Moriah. We can stand on its peak and hold on to life, or we can give God our promise, trust Him with our lives, be fruitful, and multiply!

Chapter 6

CREATIVE AUTHORITY

WHILE working in full-time ministry, my dad often used his passion for video and media as a way to share the message of the Gospel. I cannot say I have picked up on his gifting in this area, as technology is not my foremost talent. But I was able to watch him as he wrote, directed, and produced many of these videos, often watching firsthand when he enlisted me as a "D-list" actor. I will never forget the time he rented out Mile High Stadium in Denver to film a baseball scene on the Colorado Rockies' first home field. I believe I held about seven roles in that film by playing almost every position known to man. It was quite comical if you ask me. But I had no authority to say otherwise, and we were obviously a little short on good actors.

Whether I liked playing all seven of those roles or not, for my dad it wasn't funny at all. He was very gifted in directing and producing these films, and many came to Christ because of them. He produced videos all around the world as part of his calling and had a heart to grow even further in this area. Amidst all this, one thing was always important when trying to convey the message God had on his heart:

having "creative authority"—even if that authority means hiring your son for seven roles.

From what I understand, in the film business, creative authority is very sought after. This kind of authority gives you the right to control the scenes, dialogue, direction, and more, and to determine how these things impact the message. To have creative authority allows you to maintain or strengthen the quality of the message and direction and to prevent harmful compromises of the potential you are trying to reach. Basically, creative authority gives you final say over what happens and how the story moves forward.

I believe this is the kind of creative authority God gave to Adam in the Garden of Eden. It is also the kind we have increased potential to walk in because of Christ within us—much more than we even realize. We must always remain surrendered and humble before God, and we must trust Him and His will first and foremost no matter what the outcome. However, we must not let our trust make us passive or hesitant to rise up in faith to help write the story God has given us creative authority over while still in the middle of the story or scene.

> *Then God said, "Let Us make man in Our image, according to Our likeness; let them have dominion over the fish of the sea, over the birds of the air, and over the cattle, over all the earth and over every creeping thing that creeps on the earth"* (Genesis 1:26).

There have been too many days and instances when I have not fully used the faith and authority that God has given me. I have used the faith to submit to Him, to serve Him, and to join Him in the world and the lives of others; however, more creative authority has been issued to me that I have not used to the extent God desires. I have not taken full creative authority over the story God has placed before me and around me. I want to walk like Jesus, who let the Life Giver flow through Him to such an extent that He gave creative healing to disease, He calmed storms with a word, He turned water to wine, and He saw loaves and fish multiplied because He gave with Kingdom authority. I want to join Abraham, who lived and believed according to a God who *"gives life to the dead and calls those things which do not exist as though they did"* (Rom. 4:17). Abraham *"...contrary to hope, in hope believed, so that he became the father of many nations, according to what was spoken..."* (Rom. 4:18).

Adam, by faith, was called to join God in creative authority. Abraham (who is mentioned in the passage above) was called to join God in creative authority, and he did so through faith. And despite their mistakes, God birthed incredible life through these two men's direction. God is calling you and me to join Him by living out this same creative authority, perhaps to an even greater extent. We are walking in the New Covenant, a sequel to what we have read and admired of heroes like Adam and Abraham. Jesus Himself said that in the sequel we would do even greater things than the miracles we admire. We are in a sequel where all things are possible and our access has actually increased. Our authority is the same: the Life Giver still moves creatively. He is waiting for us to use what has been given, what is innately inside of us.

Right now, the Creator and Producer's Spirit is within us. Everything He would say and do if He was right here on set is inside of us. The will that God wants to accomplish with this story is waiting for us to direct. God does not want us to play seven different roles in the film because He is calling us to be more than actors. We have been called to take "dominion" or "direction" over the world and story that has been entrusted to us. Humankind gave this authority over the world back to the enemy through sin, but that authority was purchased back through the blood of Jesus Christ. We lost the authority given to us for a time, but it has been put back within us in even fuller measure.

BUT TRULY

A word I have gained much strength from declaring and repeating out loud comes from Micah 3:8, *"But truly I am full of power by the Spirit of the Lord…."* Oftentimes, the thief will use our circumstances to lie to us and make us feel like we do not have the authority that God says we do. The enemy will make us feel small in our circumstances, as if we need to run from them or even hide. *But truly*, no matter what the enemy tries to make us feel, we must *know* that we are full of power by the Spirit of the Lord.

God's creative DNA, His authority, is within us. It is there and accessible by the Spirit of the Lord. In this verse, the word *power* has many diverse meanings from which I have gleaned strength. The word *power* as defined by Strong's is *koach*, which means "vigor, strength, force, capacity, power, wealth, means, or substance."[1] So truly, we are full of *capacity* by the Spirit of the Lord. When we face a mountain in the path God has called us on, we are full of *force* by the Spirit of the Lord to see that mountain moved. When the thief tries to lie to us and tell us we do not have enough to live out God's purposes in our lives, we must remember that truly, we are *full* of wealth and means *by the Spirit of the Lord*. He lives within us, and instead of blending into or being absorbed by our circumstances, we must rise up in faith and remind our minds that truly we are full of power by the Spirit of the Lord. God wants to flow out of us in world-changing ways.

If Adam and Abraham both walked by faith in such creative and life-giving authority, what faith must we have by His Spirit within us to direct the story of the world that is before us? We have the name that is above all names and the blood that purchased it all. We are not just filling a number of acting roles; we have entered into a director's position. A role is something a person fits into, something we do far too often in the world. But a position, especially a director's position, is one that is given specifically to those who have the ability already within them and who are trusted by the Creator. God trusts us to take His story and advance it!

We already know the outcome of this story, and His Spirit lives in us to teach, guide, inspire, help, and empower. Actors without creative authority can often be put into less than desirable roles, and they can't say or do anything about it. But a director can give life to new story lines and characters to help them live out their fullest roles and potential to the end, not just for the betterment of self, but for the betterment of everyone around them. A director helps give life to the best parts of the story. The Creator/Producer has given us the script. We know what He wants, and He has promised us He will see it through. But will we step by faith from the role of actors to the entrusted position of director? God has offered us such a chair.

Abraham changed the course of life simply by believing God. Have you ever thought that one act of belief, when prompted by the Lord, could change the history of the world? Have you ever thought about what God wanted to do even when contrary to hope? The creative authority we have been given is simply to believe. If we will believe, God will unfold the rest. A character always responds to completion of whatever the director has spoken to happen. Likewise, our story and the stories of those around us will rise as high as our faith is willing to direct.

My dad did pass on some of his love for films. Though I might not know much about making one, I do love watching movies. During a movie, I enjoy remaining in a place of prayer and listening to the Lord while I watch. It is a peaceful and exciting place for me. It gets my "impossible dreams" mechanism churning with the Lord. Movies are often filled with someone who is going against the grain of the world and what would be considered conventional. They are full of impossible circumstances that must be overcome for the betterment of all. A good movie is often the story of someone who persevered by faith. The story is waiting for someone to rise up and, contrary to hope, in hope believe! So when I leave a movie theatre or a good rental, I often leave pretty fired up on the inside dreaming about how we can co-labor with God to overcome the current circumstances of the world.

Our story is much greater than any movie's. Our Producer has carved out limitless possibilities. He's asking us to both direct and act our parts and has given us the very sought-after creative authority to do so. We have creative authority over the story of our lives and the story of life on earth. We have a Creator and Producer who is guiding and teaching us, even living within us to give us creative insight. But He is waiting for us to be a people who embrace the creative authority given to us and move from a place of circumstance, which may or may not work out, and transition into a place of extraordinary hope and faith, where we watch and even direct our stories to come to pass.

> *He did not waver at the promise of God through unbelief, but was strengthened in faith, giving glory to God, and being fully convinced that what He had promised He was also able to perform. And therefore "it was accounted to him for righteousness"* (Romans 4:20-22).

Abraham believed God when it did not make sense. This brought God glory in the promise's manifestation, and Abraham was counted as righteous because of such faith. Abraham's faith extracted something unbelievable from something that did not yet exist, all because he took God at His word. Abraham was fully convinced of the promise the Creator/Producer had given him, so he used his faith to take authority and have hope over a hopeless situation.

Most box offices would be refunding a lot of tickets if the heroes in their films gave up hope, often hesitated, sometimes failed, and only occasionally succeeded. We may be acting out the roles God has placed us in, but He has given us more authority than only to act the part. We are not simply to play a role anymore, but to creatively direct the story He began called *Giving Life*. We must have faith to take hold of what *has* been given to us, and we must use this faith to give life to the places it has been stolen and to impart abundant life to those who wait to see in order to believe. The world has tickets and they are watching. They are looking to see heroes of faith rise up who will show them the story God has written and produced. This is a true story the world actually wants to be part of. They bought their tickets because they still have hope. But is this the kind of film that will cause people to believe? We have our actors, but who is directing? It is time we transition to a new position of faith and direction *with* Christ.

A FAITH'S EYE PERSPECTIVE

God is, was, and always will be the Life Giver. This is what Jesus was sent to continue, and it is what we are called to do as well. We are called to be like Christ, who took every step, every word, every action as one who could give life. If this is true, then why, I ask myself, am I so hesitant to step back from my actor's role and take the director's chair the Lord has offered? This is a place from which we can join the Life Giver in giving life.

The director's chair is not caught up in the circumstances of the story; rather, it sits back or above the scene to offer a better perspective. This faith-directing perspective is where we see beyond the immediate line or circumstance of the script. This position outside of the scene allows us to take and use the creative authority entrusted to us—and to do so from a place of increased vision. In the middle of the scene, as actors and actresses we have only a partial perspective of what is taking place. The director's seat shows a bigger picture of what is ahead. It carries the authority to alter the immediate because the director doesn't just wait for what will happen; he applies faith to what he knows is supposed to happen. Likewise, we must know the promises that God has told us *are* a part of the story. We must disengage ourselves from acting our way through the circumstances that the world throws at us and direct the scene to God's desired and promised ending.

As Christians, we believe we can have an "effect" on the world, but it should be a direct effect, where we are purposely using the creative authority God has given us to direct the story toward God's best end. He has told us the beginning. He has told us the end. And He has given us so many guidelines, principles, encouragements, promises, and keys to stay in alignment and move forward. We cannot operate by chance. Faith does not operate by chance. From the line of Adam through the life, death, and resurrection of Christ, we were created to operate as directors. We have much more direct influence on the world and the story around us than we realize. Actors have nothing but roles, but directors operate by faith. Instead of stopping at hope to believe in a possibility, we will step back and apply faith to directly influence the impossibilities we face to become not only possible with God, but certain.

WINDS AND WAVES

Have you ever been caught up in a storm of difficult circumstances? Perhaps financial pressure, relational hardship, loss, or something unexpected has suddenly left you scrambling and hoping for an answer. You may have tried everything to bring a positive resolution, but you still feel trapped and powerless in the storm. During times like these, we must remember that we have not just been called as actors, but as directors in our current scenes. Jesus gives us a great picture of the difference between the two and how to join Him in that director's role.

> Now when He got into a boat, His disciples followed Him. And suddenly a great tempest arose on the sea, so that the boat was covered with the waves. But He was asleep. Then His disciples came to Him and awoke Him,

saying, "Lord, save us! We are perishing!" But He said to them, "Why are you fearful, O you of little faith?" Then He arose and rebuked the winds and the sea, and there was a great calm. So the men marveled, saying, "Who can this be, that even the winds and the sea obey Him?" (Matthew 8:23-27)

My family and I have had a few of these "stormy" times recently. Amidst these storms, God has brought new life to this passage for me. He has not just brought new meaning to my mind, but has brought this passage to life before my very eyes. Previously, I was always an actor and the lesson was trust. I was to trust my way through the storm by knowing that Jesus was with me.

The disciples had to trust God in the midst of the storm. They needed to have peace even when life was not peaceful. The disciples had to learn that God was bigger and that they could and would keep moving forward by faith. I have watched God deliver us through many storms such as these in miraculous ways. I have learned to trust over and over again, and I will continue to learn.

However, I do not believe trust is the only lesson we are to learn from this passage. Like the disciples, we must learn to trust God. But I also believe we are called to be more like Jesus than we are like the disciples. Jesus said that we would do greater things than these (see John 14:12). We are to be like Christ—nothing less. I do not just want to be an actor in the storm learning how to be trusting and peaceful. I also want to learn to be more like Jesus so I can give life to others by giving them that same trust and peace that Jesus showed His disciples. I must not only be an actor that looks to receive peace, but a director like Jesus who gives peace in a storm.

Jesus was in the boat with His disciples. He was sitting down as an actor in the scene. But when the need or time arose, Jesus stood up. Jesus quickly went from actor to the role of a director. He stood up and rebuked the winds, and the result was a great calm. If I truly want to be more like Jesus, I must be willing to stand up. I must be willing to step beyond hope and declare my faith. If I believe God's will is to lead us through this storm, then I take authority over the storm. If I believe this storm is warfare blocking God's purposes, I must stand and command to the world that God's will be done. Neither the enemy nor the world can rise up against us and rob us, unless we allow them to. God has called us to be directors, and a director has authority over both the set and the scene. We must always remain surrendered and submitted to God, but we do not have to submit to storms.

In the Introduction of the book, I spoke of one of our daughters, Anna, whom we have adopted. I shared some of the difficulties, but also the creative solution God gave us through fresh revelation. We saw healing come to a number of layers in Anna after that first directive from the Lord. However, once this area showed healing, we began to see other layers of difficulty arise in our relationship because of the same fears and insecurities from the past.

Things were becoming very difficult again. We had little to no verbal communication, and we noticed certain things in life that were causing her to go into a paralyzed place. Whenever a particular event occurred or something specific was talked about, we saw her dive back into that dark place of depression, yielding to the thief. This time, the notebook of communication back and forth was not enough. Once again, we needed to exercise our authority as parents and give life to her by seeking God's creative solution through fresh revelation. As He had before, God was waiting for us to come to Him because He had a special answer we would not naturally go to on our own.

When we find ourselves in storms such as these, we step into the director's chair by stepping out of the circumstances mentally. When in the circumstances, we can get bogged down and lose hope. We have to position ourselves above the circumstances with an attitude of faith and expect to receive fresh revelation from God. Go somewhere away from home, take a walk, or go somewhere that allows you to breathe with God outside the box you feel you are in. When we do this, we set ourselves up to obey God's simple answer in what appears in the world to be an impossible circumstance.

This new storm with Anna was eating at our family and home once again. We were all tired from the spiritual battle being so strong, and we could feel the dark cloud come over Anna and into our house each day. It was another intense time we felt we were trying to survive. My wife was especially hurting over this struggle with Anna. Anna has such a love for her, but to almost never see it tangibly only seemed to affirm the lie of rejection.

The enemy tries to make these times so intense that we lose hope of a special answer from God. He tries to wear us down with these storms so that we won't have the strength or the time to quiet ourselves before God and hear His voice. The enemy knows that if we can still ourselves to receive something fresh from God, we will get to see God bring His word and, therefore, His solution to life. These are exactly the times we must step back from the storm, remember the power and access found in stillness with God, and await His creative answer. Once we have His creative answer, we can boldly take authority over the situation through faith and obedience.

When I finally took the time out of my "worn-out actor" mode to wait on the Lord, I was amazed how quickly God gave me fresh revelation. When I prayed for Anna, He showed me a picture of a maze. Like any maze, it had an entrance and an exit. It was full of twists, turns, dead-ends, and temporarily unseen passage ways. I saw Anna in this maze. The exit on the side opposite where she entered represented the plan God had for her life, something she knew was there. But behind her was the entrance, representing her past, and it was closer and easier to get back to. She wanted God's plan, so she started through the maze. But she would become fearful when she could not make it through on her own. Along with this fear, her pride kept her boxed in, not wanting to ask for help to the other side and risk being seen as incapable. The fear and the pride were imprisoning her and her ability to communicate. She was stuck in this box within the maze.

After praying about it further, I went to Anna to share what God had shown me. Though she had been struggling to communicate, she was usually willing to at least listen. I shared with her about the maze and the box of pride and fear. I shared about the open door at the other end of the maze leading to God's plan for her life, and she nodded her head in surprising agreement. Then I mentioned the door behind her, which was her past. "When you are afraid and can't move forward," I said, "I think this is when you look back at the past, which causes you to sink and become depressed." She nodded quietly, and my heart ached for her.

We knew Anna wanted to move forward, but this maze showed us the confusion she was caught in as to how. Many of us, or our loved ones, want to move forward, but the "how" part is where it can really seem to get overwhelming. That is why we have to leave the role of actor behind at these times—and leave the confusion along with it—while we step up into the director's chair and operate from the perspective, faith, and authority God has created us for.

I asked Anna a little more about the maze and whether or not it was accurate regarding where she was on the inside. She nodded emphatically, and she seemed genuinely surprised that God had revealed this so specifically. The vision of the maze gave us a new foundation from which to operate. No longer were we trapped upon the foundation of our circumstances, but this fresh revelation from God lifted us above the difficulties so we could see clearly again, back into a place of authority over our circumstances. We were now in position to lead Anna and ourselves peacefully through the storm to reach the other side.

At this time, we wrote out "prayer-direction" steps to get through the maze each day. These were steps and prayers she could use to take authority over her thought life that would allow her to freely move forward. Since that day, there have been far fewer days when that dark, oppressive cloud came back over her. Because of this, Anna wasn't just an actor in the maze anymore, but was learning to live from a higher perspective with more authority. God led us through a very stormy time, but we did not have that peace amidst it until we chose to step into a peace above the circumstances, and that is when we got our answer. Our answer did not just come down to us; God called us to rise higher, receive His answer, and bring that answer down to earth and our circumstances.

We have encountered similar storms with people and circumstances within our ministry. There was a very strategic time while we were living in Ethiopia, just before God brought us back to the States, when the Lord was forming our team. This was a very important time as these would be the leaders who would carry the torch moving forward. Every week something new seemed to arise with a different leader. Each individual, couple, or family had a moment of crisis or a temptation toward something that might be more secure in a worldly way. In each instance, it was not until we stepped back from enduring the storm, or trying to manage it, and stepped into a place of creative authority *with* God that we saw the Lord's peace manifested and solutions come to life. We could not enforce our will, no matter how much we wanted or tried. But each time we had to surrender the person or circumstance to God, seek His fresh revelation, declare His peace over the situation with faith, and *then* we saw even better results come to life.

I remember several times wanting to press into a situation with whoever was battling attack. However, each time God would remind me not to step into the scene or circumstance to try and bring resolution, but to step up higher to hear from Him and declare His will over the person or situation. Every single situation with every team member came to incredible conclusions. God answered each one by not only restoring what was threatened, but by giving increase to each person and his or her specific calling. It was really tempting at times to intervene and step back into the actor role. But God had something better, and I had to trust that I had more creative authority from my God-given director's chair than I did from entering the scene myself.

What difficult circumstances are before you? What seemingly impossible situation are you facing? What role do you see yourself in? Are you an actor who carries greater spiritual authority than you realized, but are perhaps being swallowed up by the storm? Or are you a director stepping back from the worldly circumstance, choosing to hear a creative word from the Lord so you can exercise your creative authority and offer His life into the situation? I have and still am learning to trust God amidst a storm like the disciples in the boat. But I cannot be who God has made me to be unless I also learn to take the director's chair that Jesus took in the same scene.

THERE IS LIFE: IN A NAME

As believers, there are so many ways we can join God in giving life to others. Not only can we give life back into difficult or hurting places, but we can creatively give new life by empowering the people and circumstances He has put before us. Our words, prayers, and blessings over others are bigger, more powerful, and carry more authority than we usually attribute to them. Each and every day, in many familiar decisions and life events, we as "directors" can set the stage for other actors/characters while they move into their next scenes. As actors, we are mostly worried about what is taking place within our roles. But as directors, we are not just living out our lives; we are creatively giving new and more abundant life to others.

Though it is God who gave me life, my mom and dad still carried a great amount of creative authority in establishing who I would become, where I would go, how I would live, and what I would do. This is true on a variety of levels, even with something as simple as my given name, Joseph. By giving me this name, my parents gave me certain blessings, affirmations, and prophetic empowerment in areas that are not always obvious or apparent at first. We give life by what we speak, and names are a great example of such. There are meanings and definitions in my name that I have seen come to life. And by calling me Joseph, my parents were calling these possibilities to life. They had creative authority to give life to specific areas of my life—whether they always intended to or not.

With our first biological daughter, Mercy, we have watched the name we gave her become very prophetic. Her heart of mercy is bigger than anything we could have drawn up had we wanted to. When we were naming her, we simply prayed about what her name was to be. We did not necessarily plan on a child whose heart overflows with mercy, but obviously that is what God had in mind, and He gave us authority as her parents to help bring His will to life.

With great authority comes great responsibility. This is why we must always return to the Word and prayer to exercise this incredible creative authority He has given us. We must partake of fresh revelation from God, which stems from His Word, and live out the creative, life-giving power He has put within us. God trusts us not only to stay in alignment and flow with His story, but to add to it with faith. God's will is always to give life. When we connect with Him for fresh revelation, the Life Giver will give that life through us creatively, even in something as simple as a name.

We mentioned the name change of our oldest adopted daughter, Anna. Her name was Kelemua, and we never had a desire to change her name. Our other adopted daughter, Aynalem, still goes by the same given name that she had when we met her. However, for Anna's

13th birthday, we were praying about something special, something that might have significance and life-changing impact. We believed God wanted to give new life to her in certain areas of her past, her present, and her future. We were praying about special ways we could bless her. But when we asked the Lord, we heard a clear message: Bless her with a biblical name change.

We sought the Lord in prayer while searching out different names and their meanings. We only came up with one possibility: *Anna*. When we looked at our daughter's spirit, we saw Anna the prophetess from the New Testament. We saw someone who was strong before the Lord in prayer and fasting, whose spirit was strong. So, just before Anna's birthday, we approached her with the name change possibility. We wanted her to feel free to receive it by faith or to decline it if it was not something that she wanted. I will never forget the moment when we asked her. I had not ever seen that much genuine excitement gush out from her. She gave us a very clear yes!

A few days later, God gave us a pretty special confirmation of this decision to bless Kelemua (now Anna) with this biblical name change. Aynalem, who had been in the same orphanage as Anna, shared something with us that Anna herself could not communicate. Apparently, Anna had secretly been praying for a new name for three months. But she wasn't praying for just any name; she had loved and wanted the name *Anna* for years up to this point—a fact we knew nothing about. A couple years earlier, someone close to her began referring to her by the very name God had recently revealed to us.

One person began speaking the biblical name of Anna over her in a casual but meaningful way. The name came to life in her heart and in her prayers. Years later, we sought the Lord, and He gave us this name without us knowing what had previously taken place. God gave new life to Anna through a new name, through a person from her past, and through new parents who asked of God for fresh revelation in the present. God wanted to give new life; we just had to join Him.

THE FATHER'S BLESSING

Personally speaking, the most powerful form of using this creative authority came from my mom and dad as they taught and imparted to me the history, lessons, and power behind the father's blessing. This is the father's blessing that began with Abraham and was passed down through Isaac and Jacob. The father's blessing began in my life when my dad asked if they could throw me a "blessing party" for my 16th birthday and encouraged me to read Genesis 27:1-40 to prepare.

> *Then his father Isaac said to him* [Jacob], *"Come near now and kiss me, my son." And he came near and kissed him; and he smelled the smell of his clothing, and blessed him and said:*
>
> *"Surely, the smell of my son is like the smell of a field which the Lord has blessed. Therefore may God give you of the dew of heaven, of the fatness of the earth, and plenty of grain and wine. Let peoples serve you, and nations bow down to you. Be master over your brethren, and let your mother's sons bow down to you. Cursed be everyone who curses you, and blessed be those who bless you"* (Genesis 27:26-29).

Isaac did not offer a blessing to Jacob from a known script. He blessed him with what God had put in his heart. Isaac blessed Jacob toward purpose, with faith, and prophesied great life to come. Now that is using creative authority. Isaac spoke life into Jacob and his future through the father's blessing. Jacob went on to live an abundantly fruitful life of purpose and impact. Isaac's blessing was more than words; it was God's power come to life because it was given with faith. Not long after this blessing and prophecy of life to come, Jacob himself had an intimate and special encounter with God at Bethel, a time we often refer to as Jacob's ladder (see Gen. 28).

When my dad approached me with this story and proposed the "blessing party" for my birthday, I must admit that I was less than enthused. I tried not to show it on the outside, but I did not initially have a lot of faith in this kind of party's potential. I was remembering back to a 13th birthday bash that I thoroughly enjoyed. We rented a rec center to accommodate more than 70 friends from youth group and school. And among other fun memories of that party, we took over the city on a widespread scavenger hunt. So, for my 16th, my fleshly perspective had me dreaming of something grand again. My mom and dad were thinking of something grand as well, but from a perspective I could not see yet. However, I could see in my dad's eyes how important this blessing party was to him, so, reluctantly, I agreed.

I read the story of Isaac, Jacob, and Esau and still did not think much of it. The night of my birthday blessing came around, and my parents had invited a number of family friends. They included a bit of an extended family from church or other families my mom and dad had been involved in ministry with for years. Everyone went around the room and took turns sharing with me. They shared memories, stories, areas of gifting, purpose, and value that they observed in my life. They spoke words of encouragement and love. It was really special. But what happened next, I will never be able to fully communicate. My parents took creative authority through their connection with God to give me new life and to speak life into the future that was ahead of me.

They had been praying for weeks, if not months, over this blessing for me. My dad wrote out a prayer of blessing that was almost three pages long. In the blessing he offered me love, belief, value, purpose, and foresight into God's potential future for my life. He blessed me to be who God had made me to be, rather than who he, my mom, or the world wanted me to be. He set me free to live the life God had purposed me for and gave me his blessing to go forward. This was huge for me, more than I even knew at the time. Like Jacob, the power of life that was injected into me at the time of the blessing has continued to be revealed more and more with each passing year. But even at that time, something changed dramatically.

I had been following the Lord at that time of my life. In fact, the year leading up to my 16th birthday was one of drawing much closer to God. He was preparing me. However, I had not been myself the previous couple years. Growing up, I was known for my energy, joy, and enthusiasm for life and others. My nickname was *Tigger* because I always bounced into a room brimming with life. But those previous couple years, though God was drawing me closer to Himself, had been marked with the death that seeps in when we care too much about what other people think and are searching for their approval.

After the blessing, this all began to change. Life started to flow again. This new or revived life came from God, but it was given through the creative authority of my parents. I had more bounce back again. But beyond that bounce, God began to give me my own prolonged "Bethel" experience like Jacob had. I began to draw very near to God, hungering and searching after God with all my heart. Life was joyful again, and I was having incredible and life-changing encounters with the Lord—encounters that have not stopped and have been increasing ever since.

This father's blessing was perhaps the most significant turn of events in my life, after my receiving Christ and the baptism of the Holy Spirit. That next year after the blessing was jam-packed with God and the overflowing of new life. However, it was also the year my dad passed away, three weeks shy of my 17th birthday, while he was on a missions trip in Vietnam. Three days before he left, I had the opportunity to return the blessing, not just as a son to a father, but while we wept hand in hand as brothers in Christ. He died unexpectedly on what was one of many frequent trips to Vietnam. But before my dad left this earth, he exercised his God-given creative authority to join the Life Giver and give me new and more abundant life. I have never been the same since that blessing, and still today, I watch new life come forward from what was given the day of the blessing. I do not know how I would have made it through my dad's sudden death if not for the life that had just been given to me.

Fourteen years ago, my dad stepped back from just being an actor in his family and in my life. He got up in the director's chair like the one he had enjoyed so frequently when making short films, and he stepped by faith into the creative authority God was calling him to use. My dad went beyond being only a disciple in the sea and storms of life and stood up to live out the life-giving nature of Christ. Ever since that day, my storm was stilled and I have been full of life!

YOU ARE FULL OF POWER!

Whatever it is that surrounds you, no matter what your circumstances try to say—remember—you are *full* of power by the Spirit of the Lord! You will see your life begin to turn the corner when you make the transition from actor to director. You have been created as a representation of the Creator. Not only have you been called, but you have been chosen—as a director—who has creative authority to give life and to give it *more abundantly*. The story is called *Giving Life,* and you are full of everything you need for the world to believe that they too have been written in to the Creator's plan.

ENDNOTE

1. James Strong, *Strong's Exhaustive Concordance of the Bible,* Hebrew #3581.

Chapter 7

PAINT THE WORLD THROUGH FAITH

…Eye has not seen, nor ear heard, nor have entered into the heart of man the things which God has prepared for those who love Him.

But God has revealed them to us through His Spirit. For the Spirit searches all things, yes, the deep things of God. For what man knows the things of a man except the spirit of the man which is in him? Even so no one knows the things of God except the Spirit of God. Now we have received, not the spirit of the world, but the Spirit who is from God, that we might know the things that have been freely given to us by God (1 Corinthians 2:9-12).

WHEN I read these verses, I see a growing vision of possibility available to us all and to the world through us. There is God's unseen Kingdom, the world of the Spirit that is full of the rich, alive, and abundant parts of God and His nature that have been freely given to us all. There is us, those who love God, upon whom and through whom He wants to bestow these awesome treasures to the world. And there is the world, people who desperately need to be shown who their life-giving Father really is. We have often painted God into a corner with our human version of His eternal love. We have painted His truths according to our context. We have drawn Him to be a worldly version of someone He very much is not. But the world is yearning for the things of God that are hidden away, the things that can't be revealed except by the Spirit, and the things that need an outlet such as us to make their way into the world. If the world will know God for the abundant life-giving Father that He is and always has been, we must learn to reveal Him in new, Spirit-led ways.

Picture this with me if you will. I see myself standing before the world with my calling to give life and life more abundantly. I see that I myself do not have enough to give unless I tap into God's life-giving Spirit who searches His true ways and nature—who wants to reveal them through us to the world. I see a black-and-white world, broken and empty from its false perceptions of who God really is. And I see a palette for painting in my hand, awaiting the new, fresh, and life-giving colors that only the Spirit of God can reveal.

Now, I have several choices in how to proceed. The world is black and white and desperately in need of color. As a Christian, I know I have a calling to bring colorful life to the world. So, I can go to the things I know best, grab my primary colors, and begin painting the world around me—a needed and wonderful thing.

Now I have to decide what kind of style to paint. I may not consider myself much of an artist, so I might be tempted to choose "paint by number," a method of painting that makes sense. It takes me through a fail-safe, proper process that will lead me to a guaranteed, but perhaps average result. What I'm saying is that probably nobody is going to stop in his or her tracks and be all that moved by what I am painting. I am using the colors that I know, colors the world has known since God painted them throughout creation and into His rainbow of promise. That rainbow was only the beginning of the promises God wants to reveal to the world. Those colors are a foundation, but the Spirit came to advance such through us. I am using a style that shows people the same pictures they have seen painted for years. So perhaps I am only deepening the need the world has to see more of who God really is.

What do I do? I must look at my artistic complement and role with the Creator in a new way. *I must paint the world through faith.* I must let Him give me new colors, colors the world has not seen before. I must take those colors, lose my paint-by-numbers sheet, tear up my fear of the unpredictable and abstract, and let my faith be a brush to the world's need. Look at verse 10 again:

> *But God has revealed them to us through His Spirit. For the Spirit searches all things, yes, the deep things of God.*

I have a palette to hold colors of paint, and I have the Spirit of God inside me. The Spirit has access to colors God has created—ways of the Kingdom and of love, forms of His grace that the world has not seen before. We do not even know them all on our own to ask for them. But the Spirit does. He is waiting for us to open up some room on our palettes to go beyond our primary colors. He is waiting for us to take our palettes of prayer and God's Word and tilt them, unafraid, toward the Spirit of God who will reveal those colors directly onto our palettes so we can partner in what God wants to reveal. The world desperately needs a revelation of who God truly is, but we cannot do this without some of the colors of God we have ignored for years.

Then, we have to break the painting open with our style and approach. God has not called us only to "paint by number." We may not consider ourselves to be artists, but God does. He has made us in His image, and He is the ultimate Creator. We have a lot more creative, life-giving ways inside us than we may know—each one of us in different and unique ways. Your creativity won't look like the person's next to you, nor should it. The world is actually longing for the unique, creative differences that God has instilled in us all. We just have to open up our style a little bit, be willing to go outside the lines, be a little more abstract and less predictable, and trust that not only can the Spirit keep us inside the lines (His lines, not ours), but He can also broaden the lines to places we didn't know they would stretch. We tend to paint by the law, but God paints with grace through faith and the power of the Spirit within us. He is looking for us to paint not just with the knowledge we know, but with the creative, love-giving explosion He has placed within our hearts. Do our children have to paint a masterpiece for us to put it on our fridge? Neither does God expect a masterpiece from us; He just wants us to paint with the freedom of the Spirit—and faith.

RAW, OUTSIDE-THE-LINES EXPRESSION

One of my favorite stories in the Bible is of Mary's encounter with Jesus at Bethany. It was six days before Passover, and Jesus was sitting with His disciples, Lazarus, Mary, and Martha. The following account, to me, is the perfect picture of how the Lord wants our faith to lead us. Mary did something that had no practical sense or reason. But her actions were full of faith, and she was allowing that faith to spill out over the world all around her, even if it meant going outside the lines.

> *Then Mary took a pound of very costly oil of spikenard, anointed the feet of Jesus, and wiped His feet with her hair. And the house was filled with the fragrance of the oil. But one of His disciples, Judas Iscariot, Simon's son, who would betray Him, said, "Why was this fragrant oil not sold for three hundred denarii and given to the poor?"*

...But Jesus said, "Let her alone; she has kept this for the day of My burial. For the poor you have with you always, but Me you do not have always" (John 12:3-5;7-8).

Mary may not have painted the world with her faith, but she spilled her life all over it, practically doing the same. Mary's worship and action was *raw*. It was not something that was a ritual or a tradition, and according to Judas, she did not stay inside the lines. Her action was not proper, and you might actually say (Judas did) that it did not make good financial sense. It was *raw* faith. This is what pleased Jesus so much. He didn't care about wearing the costly oil. He didn't care about what it would do for Him. He just wanted her raw, faith-painted expression of love.

And do not be conformed to this world, but be transformed by the renewing of your mind, that you may prove what is that good and acceptable and perfect will of God (Romans 12:2).

We often want to take what God has taught, shown, or put inside us and carefully let it leak out on the world in a refined way. But God is not looking for those whose minds are refined; God is searching for creative life-givers whose minds are renewed.

I know my children didn't start out painting *inside* the lines. And I sure did not expect them to. I wanted them to have fun, knowing very well the quality of their work would come over time. That is what I love about the word *renewed*. It is so easy to see that word reading through Romans 12:2 and assume it means "changed." It does not mean changed. God is calling us to be made new again, like when we were children—that time in life when we painted bright, newly-invented colors outside the lines and even occasionally on the wall. In fact, I can recall cleaning up several of those "masterpieces." My daughter drew one just the other day.

We must not allow the presence of a couple messes here and there to cause us to substitute our daily renewing of the mind with refining ourselves from the mind. Renewal happens by grace, and therefore, renewal lives and functions through the presence of grace. But refining relies heavily upon the law (the lines) and works (paint by number). Too often we are becoming refined life-protectors who need to be transformed into renewed life-givers.

We are transformed by the *renewing* of our mind so that we can go forward and approve God's good, perfect, and acceptable will. I do not believe it is God's will for us to constantly live in a paint-by-number, primary color world. There is too much more of Himself He wants to reveal, and He wants to reveal it through us. Eye has not seen, nor ear heard those things that God has prepared for those who love Him. However, He does want to reveal those deep things. He does want us to go and approve the Kingdom-oriented colors that have been hidden away for far too long. But for us to go forward and approve these amazing, God-revealing colors to the world, we must first start painting like children again, through grace-filled, childlike faith.

We must be made new again. To give life as God has called us to, we can't put such firm clamps on our brushes. We can't think too hard. I'm an even worse artist than usual when I think hard about what I am doing. I have to free myself from thinking so hard and putting up that filter of self. We often make ourselves filters for what parts of God get through to the world. But isn't it supposed to be the other way around? Aren't we supposed to trust the Spirit to be a filter for us? He is perfectly capable, much more so than us. He knows our hearts and intentions. And He wants truth and love expressed purely even more than we do. Let's face it: the Spirit is better at staying in control and within the lines than we ever try to be. He can see the same lines we're trying to stay within. He wants us to feel free, to be creative, and to take what God is waiting to reveal to us and reveal it to the world. God has put things inside us that need to come out just as they were put in. Our good intentions, cautions, and refined, proper living are noble, but through such things we have put the clamps on God's power and His creativity.

God is much more creative than we give Him credit for. His ways and thoughts far exceed those that we possess. What the world needs is to experience *who* God really is. For this to happen, we must allow ourselves to experience who God really is. We can't be afraid of mistakes or failure from the world's view, as long as we are being obedient to God. The colors of God are much different from the ones we have grown up with. They are much brighter and more full of life than we know. In fact, God's deep and hidden colors are full of life *more* abundantly!

ACCESSING GOD'S "OTHER" COLORS

If we are to see the palette God has given us full of new and heavenly colors, we have to make ourselves available to it. We have to acknowledge our need for more than we already have. I remember when God began to take me to very new places with Him when I was 17 and 18 years old. I didn't know what I was getting into, and I wasn't in control of my journey, but I was surrendered, and that's all God needed to take care of the rest. He gave me revelation, visions, and dreams that my family and I are only now beginning to see come forward. He taught me things and imparted Kingdom principles to me that I didn't even know existed and didn't know how to ask for. All I knew was that I needed more. I needed colors that I couldn't concoct. I needed to learn His ways above my own. I needed more of God and nothing less. The word *more* became one of my favorite words. In all other parts of my life, I learned to become more content, but as far as God was concerned, I just wanted *more*.

I remember many prayer times deep in the basement—my room at the time—where I fell on my face and surrendered. I needed what only He could give. I didn't know the deep things I was asking for, nor could I perfect my understanding of them. I could seek out wisdom and counsel to help make sense of them, but first I had to get His new colors before I could try to understand them. I needed life that went beyond what people could give me. I dove into His Word for my foundation, and I cried out over and over, "Lord, pour into me the things I don't even know how to ask for. Speak to me. Teach me!" And He did.

That was one of the most amazing times of my life. I am only now starting to understand some of what He was revealing to my spirit then. He filled me, He healed me, and He prepared me. He gave me more of Him by giving me direct revelation of Himself, His ways, His strategies, His heart, and His purposes.

> That the God of our Lord Jesus Christ, the Father of glory, may give to you the spirit of wisdom and revelation in the knowledge of Him, the eyes of your understanding being enlightened; that you may know what is the hope of His calling, what are the riches of the glory of His inheritance in the saints, and what is the exceeding greatness of His power toward us who believe, according to the working of His mighty power (Ephesians 1:17-19).

Before I could give life and paint the world through faith, I had to learn how to access those deep, hidden colors of God that only His Spirit could reveal to me. I was blessed with many, many wonderful people around me who imparted all kinds of wisdom. But God wanted me to know the value of revelation—not only what it would mean to me, but what it would mean to the world through me. As Christians, called to be life-givers, we are the conduit between the Life Giver Himself and those who so desperately need more life.

Revelation is one of the greatest tools we can use to access those new colors of God, and revelation by the Spirit will also show us where, when, and how to apply that paint to the world.

Wisdom is practical in nature and is something that can be passed down from one person to another. Wisdom is a bit like the primary colors. We need them. The new colors do not come forward without such. Wisdom is *vital* in our daily walks with the Lord and with one another. But because wisdom stems from past experiences and understanding and is easier to grasp, it is much easier to rely on than revelation.

Receiving revelation requires a value for the fresh insight that God pours out or gives in a new way, situation, or time. Revelation helps us to step into the new things of God. This is not to say that we should value revelation over wisdom. However, it is to say that because of the nature of wisdom, we can very easily fall out of balance and overvalue wisdom in relation to revelation, or vice versa. The two should work together more equally. We should walk in such a way that wisdom and revelation have the opportunity to carry equal weight into all areas of our lives and choices. But that is not always the case. Wisdom may provide a history of past colors that have worked in bringing new life to the world, but only through revelation by the Spirit can we receive that which the world longs for this very day and in the days to come. Just because God used the primary colors in the rainbow does not mean those are the only colors He knows—perhaps they are simply the only colors *we* have yet received.

THE GIFT THAT KEEPS ON GIVING

Words have always come pretty easily to me, as has communicating my heart to others. I have always been a "wear my heart on my sleeve" kind of guy. So, when it comes to writing a card to someone close to me and sharing words of love and encouragement, it is not usually a difficult task.

However, I remember one Mother's Day when I could not find any words. My mom has been such a life-giver in my life, and in many others'. She has modeled and led me into intimacy with the Lord since a very young age. Usually, I could bless her in a card by just sharing my heart and how much she means to me and to others on so many levels. But that Mother's Day, words just did not seem enough. I wanted to bless her for who she was and all that she had poured into me.

I began to ask God to show me. I needed God to reveal to me how I could bless her. As I prayed, the Spirit brought back to memory a phrase I had heard her utter to my sister and me thousands of times, a phrase I'm sure many parents have spoken or wanted for their children: "I wish I could give you all you could ever need."

She had said it so many times, and for her, it was not something she simply said, but it was something she truly meant with every part of her. And that's when the Lord showed me how I could bless her, what I could say to let her know all she had given me. I could tell her that she had done it: She truly had given me all I could ever need, just as she had always hoped for. Now, I understand that this might sound a bit crazy to some. As no one person can or should meet all our needs. But you see, my mom had taught me and shown me how to wait on God and hear His voice. She had taught me how to stand on the Word of God and get fresh revelation from Him each day. I had come to the conclusion that if we know how to listen to God, there is no more we could ever need. We know when to go to the left, and we know when to go right. We know when to stop, when to sit still and be patient, when to step boldly, when to persevere, and when to give freely. If I know how to listen to God, there is nothing I could ever need.

So, in my heart and mind, she had done it! My mom had given me everything I could ever need in this world because she taught me how to listen to God. That is what I wrote to her on that Mother's Day card. "Mom, you've done it. You have given me everything I could or will ever need. You taught me how to listen to God, and because of that, you have changed my life forever."

IMPACTING OTHERS, GIVING LIFE

This kind of fresh revelation not only gives life to us, but it brings us the heavenly abundant life we are to give the world, and it's where we learn strategy and timing for how to give that life outwardly. If I know how to listen to God, not only do I have everything I could ever need, but I have everything I could ever need to give. For someone who is called with Christ to give life and give it more abundantly, that is a pretty powerful gift.

Every word we speak can give life as a seed. Each word, or seed, contains a love that never fails. All that each seed of love waits for is for us to apply the pressure of faith. From faith that love-seed sprouts up and brings life more abundantly! When we tap into the Life Giver for Him to reveal the depths of His love expressed through words, we can paint life into a person with a color he or she never knew existed, let alone one that existed upon and within them.

Hebrews 11:3 states:

> *By faith we understand that the worlds were framed by the word of God, so that the things which are seen were not made of things which are visible.*

I love this word! "*The things which are seen were not made of things which are visible.*" I want to live like this more often! God shows us the model of being a Life Giver who gives life to something or someone that does not yet exist. He is in the business of birthing! We often want to wait and see something before we will offer our faith to approve it. However, God wants us to use our faith to tap into Him, allow His Spirit to reveal to us how He sees something or someone before that life exists, and then help that new life come into existence. My favorite example of this is in giving life to others through prophetic blessings.

In the previous chapter, I wrote about the blessing that my dad and mom gave me on my 16th birthday. That blessing changed my life. It was a blessing and impartation that gave me life. Now that same blessing is something God has been teaching me to impart to others. This blessing is a big part of the foundation of the movement God began a few years back in Ethiopia and in other nations we traveled to as well. More than speaking to a group, our desire is for God to show a group who they are in His eyes so they can find His vision and purpose for their lives and walk in the hope of their calling in Christ.

Before moving to Ethiopia, God had connected us with a small orphanage that was more like a children's family home than a typical orphanage. The first time we arrived, we walked through the rickety wooden gate and started to hug the children, and all I could see was that this was "God's house of treasure." The world saw orphans and a beat up house and compound. But God saw light, value, and treasures that were overflowing lives, ripe for redemption.

As soon as we moved to Addis Ababa, we began to go to this children's home once a week just to get to know the kids, hug them, love on them, and ask God to help us see them as He saw them. After about a month of this, we arranged for the kids (eight of them at the time) to come over to our house for a "Pray & Play Weekend." The focus of the weekend was to have the kids for a few nights and enjoy time together, but we also had begun preparing a father's blessing for each of the "orphans"—kids that God saw as way more than orphans.

We had spent weeks praying over each child and asking God to give us revelation of how He saw him or her. We asked God to show us their gifts, their designed personalities, their talents, and their purposes and calling. We asked God to show us their past wounds and how He wanted to speak love and healing into those places. I had done this for a number of people since the blessing God gave me through my mom and dad. But there was something new and different at work here in another nation, through a new language, and with those the world might see as the most broken. God was calling them out to more!

With help from those who became our Ethiopian family, we got each blessing translated, printed, fitted with a photo, and framed. We couldn't wait to start; we wanted so badly to see God speak new, fresh, abundant life over and into these kids. Saturday night came, the night of the blessings, and we brought everyone into our dining room. I shared a little of my testimony regarding my dad, the blessing he gave me, and how it changed my life and gave me life. We talked about the history, value, and power of the blessing with Abraham, Isaac, and Jacob. These kids, aged 6 to 11 at the time, sat in complete silence and focus. To be honest, we were pretty amazed at that part.

We began with the oldest boy and continued in order of age. We called him forward and told him we wanted to give him a similar blessing from God as my dad had given me. We told him that we had been praying for him and asking God to reveal His heart for this boy's life. This young man had been going through a bit of an extra rocky time during the months leading up to this night. He had been wavering in attitudes and decisions, which showed us even more how much he was longing to know God's heart over him. We handed him the frame and then began reading and praying the blessing over him in English and Amharic one sentence at a time.

From the beginning of the blessing, this young man's countenance began to change. His head, his eyes, and his posture were transitioning from shame to light. We finished declaring this blessing over him and asked the kids to go around the room and speak to this boy about what they saw of God in his life. Eight-year-old girls began speaking life into him. At this point, he was now being valued and affirmed by his peers. Life began to well up in him. It was now spilling out! The kids joined us in laying hands on him as we closed in a time of prayer, declaration, and blessing. God poured out on him during that time. As life arose in him, the places the thief once held were refilled and life more abundantly took their place. I will never forget seeing the change in him and on him immediately. He rose up as a leader in a new way. For every blessing to every child after him, he helped lead the way. He began speaking life and giving life to the purposes, gift-ings, and calling that was in each of his brothers and sisters. He was no longer someone who was receiving ministry, but he took hold of the new life breathed into him and began to pass it on as quickly as he could.

This night of blessing with each of these kids was something I will never forget. The revelations God gave us over each child gave them new life—and brought amazing life to us as well.

What is so awesome is that this new life did not stop giving with the kids or our family. We began to meet with these kids every week for a prayer time. However, our prayer time wasn't what most would imagine. Instead of praying together, we spent most of our time wait-ing on God together. We gave each child a "God Journal" that he or she could seek God with all week long. We told them to take full liberty with their journals, whether it was drawing something God showed them, reciting a promise from His Word that He gave them, or praying whatever He had put on their hearts. We just asked that the journals be an open dialogue of two-way communication with the Lord.

Each week, we came back together and asked the kids to teach us and one another with what God had spoken to them. The life inside them continued to rise up and flow out. One week, we presented them with the vision of all the other street children across Ethiopia who had grown up experiencing similar pain and bondage as they had, but who had not had the chance even to go into an orphanage or children's home. We asked the kids a couple questions: How do you think God sees them? What do you think God wants to say to them? We asked them to write letters to the street children across Ethiopia based on what the Spirit spoke to their hearts as they prayed about these questions. We wanted these kids to see their peers as God saw them.

These eight kids came back to us with incredible prayers, answers, and words of life and love. We took all these letters and combined them into one original blessing that we could give to street children as we met them on the street. Now the kids would not only be receiving love and hope from us, but from kids their own age who, despite similar circumstances, were living life more abundantly. We saw many kids from the street come to know the Lord through this blessing written by orphans—because they waited on God for revelation of how God wanted to paint life into those in need. The age of these eight orphans did not matter; nor did their life circumstances disqualify them. In fact, their life circumstances were a testimony that brought great authority of life. These kids were not even limited by what they did or did not have. They had the Lord. He had revelation, love, and life to give, and these kids were willing to be part of giving it out.

This is the life we can pass on to people around us every day. However, such life is not possible without the life that comes from revelation from the Spirit of God. Those kids were painted with new and vibrant colors that night, colors that only God knew to give. Those colors weren't on our palette until we turned it toward the Spirit and asked Him to reveal the things that He had planned for these kids. We had to see them like God sees them, as Heaven's promises look down on them. We had to give faith, hope, and love to them according to what was on God's palette instead of what was on ours. Once we received that life to give, it was up to us to start painting through faith. And as God gave life to these kids through us, not only did we see fruit, but we saw these once hurting, orphaned children begin to multiply life to others just like them.

RENEWED, CREATIVE ARTISTS

If we are going to be more effective givers of life, we must learn to be more *renewed* than *refined*. I am compelled by the Lord to let go of the refined lines I paint within, be renewed to childlike faith and painting, and go outside of *my* lines to paint more freely and fully within God's. This freedom wouldn't be possible except by the Spirit inside me. I have refined colors that are only foundations. I have lines on my paper that are only a small part of God's vision. His lines must become my lines and His colors my colors. When this happens, I can give life and paint the world through faith with the Creator Himself.

More than a refined painter, I want to be a renewed life-giver. I want to tap into the love that is beyond the love I know and carry. And I want to declare that love, hope, and purpose, through faith, all over the world around me, to the people who are dying to know the Father's true colors.

We must become like a child. We must believe like a child. We must love like a child. We must see the best in everyone, like a child. We must begin painting again, like a child. Only then will our worship of the Lord extend out to give life to those around us and become more than a refined human effort. We must turn our palette to the Spirit of the Lord and allow Him to give us the colors the world is waiting for. It will become a raw explosion of free and colorful love, drawing life out of God's children and empowering them to live and give life more abundantly. Let's paint the world—through faith!

Chapter 8

THE OTHER SIDE OF THE BOAT

FOR a number of years, I have frequently stared at the story in John 21 about Jesus, His disciples, and their experience while fishing that night. The story draws me because I want to fish with the Lord on "the other side of the boat." I want more of God! As mentioned earlier, the word *more* has characterized my prayers for years, and this passage describing a fishing trip shows me an instance of crossing over into a powerful catch of "more." I can't stand the thought of not walking with the Lord into all He created me for, and I want to leave nothing on the table. That is what I pray for each child of God. My heart breaks at the thought of my own humanness limiting any amount of love or fruit God might birth through me. I realize my need for more of God. And when I am more full of His love, I will love Him more and have more love to live and life to give. When I read this story from John 21, I always see our opportunity for more. I want to live and fish from "the other side of the boat." That is where Jesus is calling us.

What is "the other side of the boat"? To find out, we have to go fishing, both in the natural and the supernatural. The disciples were fishermen, but they were called to be "fishers of men." I see a group of those who had been called, but who were now stepping into the fullness of who God had created them to be. This group of disciples and fisherman went from professional fishermen who caught nothing that night to fishermen with a great catch. I believe we see a spiritual parallel begin to take its course after this story in the rest of John 21 and in the Book of Acts thereafter. But first, the big fish story.

A NEW KIND OF FISHING

Simon Peter said to them, "I am going fishing." They said to him, "We are going with you also." They went out and immediately got into the boat, and that night they caught nothing.

But when the morning had now come, Jesus stood on the shore; yet the disciples did not know that it was Jesus. Then Jesus said to them, "Children, have you any food?" They answered Him, "No."

And He said to them, "Cast the net on the right side of the boat, and you will find some." So they cast, and now they were not able to draw it in because of the multitude of fish (John 21:3-6).

When I look at this story in John 21, I see fishermen who crossed over into the "more" of God. God had called them to more from the beginning, but now they were beginning to experience it to a new and heightened degree.

These were professional fishermen; fishing was how they made their living. They knew what they were doing, and one night, they went out to do it. However, the night passed without these professional fishermen catching a thing. Not one fish! This is when Jesus showed up to help them cross over and transition to something more. This is when Jesus appeared to them; however, at that time they still did not know it was the Lord. This voice called to the disciples from the shore and suggested they cast their net on the right side of the boat, and it let them know they *would* find some.

This must have sounded crazy! But maybe they were just hitting that point of being desperate enough to try something that defied common sense. Number one, they were professional fishermen, and they had no idea who was giving them this suggestion. And number two, they had fished all night on the left side of the boat and caught nothing. Were they really supposed to believe that tossing their net a mere 20 feet to the right would make *that* much of a difference? In typical terms, it would not make this big of a difference at all. But the "right" side of the boat was more than a specific location: it symbolized crossing over into something new. The disciples were changing their vision, as slight as the change may have seemed. Such a slight transition of obedience can mean everything when doing so *with* the Lord.

The disciples were desperate enough for something more that they made this seemingly ridiculous change, listened to the bystander on the shore, and moved their net slightly to the other side of the boat. We are told that this simple change caused reality to defy the impossible, and the disciples' net became so full that they were not able to draw it in because of the abundance of fish. In fact, the catch was so great that later in the passage when they were preparing to partake of this provision, the disciples found themselves shocked. They were amazed at the fact that, though there were so many fish, the net still was not broken.

Jesus said to them, "Bring some of the fish which you have just caught." Simon Peter went up and dragged the net to land, full of large fish, one hundred and fifty-three; and although there were so many, the net was not broken (John 21:10-11).

First, these fishermen had a supernatural catch, going from zero fish all night to 153 in what must have felt like a moment. Then, their net held up against what they previously may have considered to be overwhelming circumstances. These professional fishermen were taught how to fish in a new way, according to a new strength. Less work, less striving, *more* abundance! They transitioned, even in their natural occupation, to the "other" side of the boat. They went from professional fishermen to supernatural fishermen in the blink of an eye.

I can remember many times over the past ten years when I have felt like I was fishing on the left side of the boat. I could utilize all my natural talents, and even diligently work from my spiritual gifts, yet could still fish a whole night without catching a thing. Where was the provision? Where was the fruit? God had promised much more. That's when God would take me back to this passage and remind me how ever so close the right side of the boat really was. He would show me little things in my life each time, such as wrong perspectives or strife, that were slight counterfeits to the ways of God and countered the freedom and strength of His love. Each time I wanted it, God wanted to give me the "more" on the other side of the boat even more than I wanted to receive it. And therein lay the problem: I wanted so badly to find His more that sometimes I would forget to receive the more that was waiting to be walked in.

The disciples' transition from ordinary fishermen to supernatural, abundant fishermen is not the only transition I see taking place in John 21. Not only were the disciples fishermen, but when they began to follow Jesus, they were called to be "fishers of men." They had followed Jesus all this time as "fishers of men" who caught almost nothing themselves. They watched Jesus catch a lot, but they themselves were like "fishers of men" who had gone the whole night fishing on the left side of the boat. God had called them to more than they were currently walking in, and just as Jesus had led them to new ground in their professional calling, He also wanted to take them to the other side of the boat in their spiritual calling.

Just after their "big fish story" at the beginning of John 21, the disciples began this greater transition with the Lord, crossing over in their heavenly calling to the other side of the boat where there would be far more than 153 fish awaiting them. This crossing over of sorts is amped up a level in this same chapter of John 21, right after their fishing trip, when Jesus began to call Peter to the other side of the boat.

OUR "NET" OF LOVE

In my Bible, the subtitle for this story of Jesus and Peter's conversation reads, "Jesus Restores Peter." I think this is an important word—*restores*. It would be easy to see this conversation unfold and think that Jesus was rebuking Peter. And this may be an easy assumption, as we have seen in the Gospels several prior circumstances where Jesus did need to rebuke Peter. But in this passage, I do not see a rebuke; I see Peter being restored through a challenge rather than a rebuke.

> So when they had eaten breakfast, Jesus said to Simon Peter, "Simon, son of Jonah, do you love Me more than these?" He said to Him, "Yes, Lord; You know that I love You." He said to him, "Feed My lambs." He said to him again a second time, "Simon, son of Jonah, do you love Me?" He said to Him, "Yes, Lord; You know that I love You." He said to him, "Tend My sheep." He said to him the third time, "Simon, son of Jonah, do you love Me?"

Peter was grieved because He said to him the third time, "Do you love Me?" And he said to Him, "Lord, You know all things; You know that I love You." Jesus said to him, "Feed My sheep" (John 21:15-17).

I do not believe Jesus is actually questioning Peter's love; rather, I believe He is challenging Peter's love to rise higher. But at the time, Peter obviously did not see it that way. The passage even describes Peter as "grieved." But, God knows where He is taking us. We often take the moment for what it appears to us, but God brings us a moment to lead us to maximize the future He is leading us into. Jesus knew Peter loved Him, but Jesus also knew that Peter's love needed to be revived and called to rise higher if he was to walk in the calling and the season that was just ahead.

As we talked about before, Peter had been called with the other disciples to be "fishers of men." However, even though Peter was following Christ, he wasn't yet personally living out that calling. Peter was fishing on the left side, and he needed to cross over to the other side of the boat in his own calling as a "fisher of men." I believe this is a big part of what Jesus was looking at. Jesus knew what Peter would be called to during the time that we would later know as the Book of Acts and beyond that time. Jesus knew that Peter needed to start living on the other side of the boat, so He had to challenge him in a way that would help him cross over, not only as a supernatural fisherman this time, but as a supernatural "fisher of men."

What we know as the Gospels of Christ—Matthew, Mark, Luke, and John—were like Peter's spiritual left side of the boat. Our hindsight allows us to see the Book of Acts in a way that represents Peter's "right side" of the boat. As a "fisher of men," Peter caught nothing in the Gospels all night long. But suddenly, in the Book of Acts, God brought in a catch through Peter and the disciples far greater than the 153 the fishermen caught that night. Peter had to transition from the left side of the boat (how he lived in the Gospels) to the right side of the boat (how he lived in the Book of Acts). In this conversation with Peter in John 21, Jesus was calling Peter to transition to live out his calling in a supernatural way, a way that was bigger than himself. To spark this transition, Jesus chose to challenge Peter's *love*. After this challenge, Peter and the other disciples found a catch on the other side of the boat they never could have dreamed of the night before. Jesus' challenge of Peter was akin to Jesus' question to the fishermen the night before: "Have you any food?" Now He was asking, "Do you love Me?" Jesus knew the answer to both questions when He asked them, but He wanted to light a fire that would cause them to cross over to the fullness of the supernatural life for which God created them.

What I love about this challenge isn't just the challenge itself; I *love* that the challenge was all about *love*. Jesus knew Peter could not walk in the other side of his calling until his love had been revived and caused to rise higher. A revived, strengthened, new love was required of Peter to cross over into God's desired calling for him. So Jesus challenged Peter's love. Then He challenged it again. And then He challenged it again! When Jesus was convinced that Peter's *love* was strong enough to support his calling, like the net that stood the test of 153 fish, then Peter was released to walk in the other side of his calling. But it was not until love took him there. Peter could not have lived out the life he lived in the Book of Acts without a revived, strengthened, and restored love. Jesus is challenging us all to walk in a new kind of love—a level of love that will propel us to the other side of the boat.

REVIVE MY LOVE

I want to tell you the story of an impossible battle that revived my love and took Destiny and me to "the other side of the boat." By *impossible battle* I do not at all mean that the primary person involved in this story was impossible. He was, and is, precious! Rather, God put Destiny and me in an impossible circumstance that He never meant for us to win, but one He used to revive, transform, and reform us while we were seemingly lost.

Over the years I have often heard people share a long-standing illustration where God gives someone a 10,000-pound boulder and instructs them to *push*. The person pushes and pushes without ever moving that boulder even an inch. After all, it weighs 10,000 pounds.

At first that person may feel like a failure and in need of grace. But he or she later realizes God never intended him to *move* the impossible boulder, just to *push*. God knew the calling on that person's life where he would soon be called on to *move* a 5,000-pound boulder. When the person reaches this slightly smaller, but still seemingly impossible work, he suddenly finds that due to all his previous, heavy, fruitless pushing, now he can push something that would have seemed impossible. The impossible 10,000-pound challenge to *push* strengthened and prepared him.

A couple years back, we faced an impossible, 10,000-pound boulder. Every day not only did we push, but it pushed back—hard. However, this "boulder" also pushed us to a new level of our calling, to a greater love than we ever would have known without it—a love that later could begin moving 5,000-pound boulders.

This is the story of Sidamo, Samuel, and Micah. Three stories, but one child of God. For us, it's a story of a big, impossible boulder, immense grace, a lot of perseverance, revived love, and *the other side of the boat*. Again, I want to be clear: This is in no way to say that this precious child was an impossible task. Rather, the task the Lord put before us at a specific time in his life, mixed with the time in our lives, was a 10,000-pound boulder on which we pushed, and pushed, and dug deeper, and pushed some more. Turns out, we weren't supposed to move that boulder, just push. God moved it, and this precious boy, as well as us, moved on to the boulders we were actually called to move.

SIDAMO

Sidamo was an Ethiopian infant. He was born two months premature in a rural, down-country area. As if it wasn't enough to battle this world as a two-month premature infant, Sidamo was thrown and abandoned in a field.

Eventually, Sidamo was discovered by the police, who took him in to a nearby orphanage for care. Despite his incredibly special needs, the trauma he underwent, and his premature size, which all went largely uncared for, Sidamo was matched with a prospective adoptive family. They had been waiting for God to place a young infant in their family. However, Sidamo's needs were immense, and when the social workers found that Sidamo's new family were soon to be missionaries, the adoption process was shut down for fear that Sidamo's extreme case may be too much for a family in such a precarious state of their lives.

Sidamo was now in the system, but without a family. He was being cared for at a new transition home for orphans who are awaiting their families' arrival. However, since the adoption fell through, Sidamo was at this home without any hope of a family arriving soon.

My family and I were living in Addis Ababa at the time, and we were also awaiting the conclusion of our own adoption process for our two older girls, Anna and Aynalem. During the specific time of Sidamo's birth, we were actually in the United States visiting family, mission partners, and churches and preparing the paperwork for our adoption to be completed once we arrived back in Ethiopia. During our trip to the States, we had felt a burden to be praying for families for the rest of the kids at the children's home that our daughters were coming from. We were so close to all the kids, and all held such a special place in our hearts. We traveled around the U.S. with pictures of them all and stories to tell, and we prayed with potential families who were considering adoption. This time really strengthened our relationship with a lot of new families, and these relationships have blessed our lives considerably.

We were especially praying for one particular boy, the oldest at the home. Being the oldest boy, we couldn't bear the thought of other kids leaving the home without the same hope being alive in him. We weren't hearing of anything happening for him, so we continued to pray. About two weeks before we were going to leave for home in Ethiopia, God prompted our hearts to commit to focused prayer and fasting for a week in faith that God would raise up a family for him. A couple other families who knew this awesome young man joined us in the fast that week, and we believed God together for His answer.

I will never forget a morning at the end of the week. I was in the shower seeking the Lord in prayer. Finally I asked Him, "Lord, are You going to do this and raise up a family for this boy?"

He spoke to my heart as clear as day, "Will you let your heart be made keen to another?"

"Yes," I answered back immediately. I had no idea what the Lord was asking of me at that time, which was a little scary, but yes, of course, my heart is the Lord's and whatever He says, I'm in.

Nothing more happened immediately toward this older boy or as far as our hearts being made keen to another. We traveled back to Ethiopia and were just settling in our first couple days back when our adoption worker from the States came to help us prepare our paperwork and do our home study. The time went well and all the preparation for our adoption was moving forward accordingly. Then, just before she was about to leave, she began to tell us about two special-needs babies in the transition home who desperately needed care.

The transition home was being filled up quickly, and the staff members and nannies had full plates. Therefore, they had a very difficult time caring for two highly special-needs children who did not yet have families. As she began to relay the need, my heart was just a little jumpy, a little excited, but very nervous that one of these children was who the Lord spoke to me about a couple weeks before when asking if we would allow our hearts to be made keen to another. Still, I was all in with what the Lord was doing, and I genuinely wanted to love one or both of these children in need. However, our second daughter had recently been born and was now 9 months old. One of our adopted daughters was preparing to come begin her life in our family within three weeks, and I did not want to take in another child only out of emotion. We had to know God was in it. I wanted to make sure we were wise, but mostly that we were obedient, because this would be a large, unexpected step of faith.

My heart was already processing what might be coming when the woman asked if we would be willing to take one of these children into our home until God raised up a family. We knew what the Lord had spoken to us recently while praying for the older boy at the children's home, but we wanted to make sure. We knew the timing was desperate, so we asked for just a day or two to seek the Lord and know this was from Him for this time.

We prayed, called others to prayer, and were on our faces before the Lord all day and night. We felt a "yes" from the Lord that one of the children she mentioned, a highly special-needs, premature infant boy, needed to be in our home. In fact, Destiny had experienced a dream about six months earlier of a small infant boy being dropped off at our home. However, we were also terrified at the time. We sensed a clear go-ahead from God, but we also felt the gravity of the situation. I believe our hearts knew that it was the right thing, but that it would not be an easy thing. We continued to war over this in our spirits, not wanting to compromise our family or anything God may have planned for the season. However, we thought, *Maybe this boy is what God has planned for this season, and we are simply to welcome him and love him like family.*

The next morning we woke up and felt the urgency to give our final answer. I went to get on email, as our electrical power and Internet had been out the whole day before when our adoption worker was visiting. As soon as I logged on, I had every confirmation we needed that we were to say yes to this needy, but precious little baby boy. I opened an email that was sent during the exact hour when the adoption worker asked us whether we would be willing to care for this baby in our home. The email was from a family we had just spent time with in the U.S. They wrote to tell us that God had confirmed something in their hearts: they were to adopt the oldest boy from the children's home, the same boy for whom we were fasting and praying when the Lord asked us if we would allow our heart to be made keen to another. I don't know if we could have gotten a clearer confirmation from God.

We called immediately to say we would gladly welcome this young baby boy into our home. The coordinators of the transition home did not know what this premature baby's primary issues were, except that he was very small (only a couple pounds), very sick, and in need of love. Within a day, this little boy, Sidamo, arrived at our home. Our hearts broke to see how small and how sick he was. He appeared to be just on the edge of life, a delicate flower starved of water, light, or roots to grow from. He was so fragile we worried for his ability to make it through the night. Here in the States, he likely would have been in ICU with tubes to feed him and help him breathe. In Ethiopia, love and grace were his only chance. Love and grace were our only chance as well. God's grace was all we had. But His grace, no matter how difficult the situation, is *always* sufficient. Welcome, Sidamo!

SAMUEL

When Sidamo arrived with our family, all we could do was call on the grace of God. None of the circumstances of our natural lives lined up with his arrival, but God's desire was evident: We were to simply love him.

Love is all we had. This precious little boy could barely sleep. His stomach really wrestled against him, causing him to hunger deeply because he could not retain food—so much so that he would cry for food at the same time he cried for it to be taken away. His body was brittle, and he could barely move his limbs. From the moment he arrived, he would have terrifying panic attacks, sometimes one every other minute. They were neither seizures nor just fits of discomfort; rather, Sidamo appeared terrified during these attacks, as if he was being tormented by the devil himself. We had never witnessed anything to this extent before, let alone with an infant.

We had no medical background or experience. But we had love. And every day, as the difficulties actually grew in those first four months with Sidamo, it felt like through this little baby, Jesus was asking us the same challenging question that He asked Peter over and again: "Do you love Me?" Every day we pleaded for the Lord to revive, strengthen, and deepen our love. Our love was not enough; we needed His love to care for this special little boy.

We used what we had in our hands and, even more, what we had in our hearts. But as we found out time and time again, even what we had in our hearts was not enough. Sidamo needed more. Sidamo needed love that could not come from humans alone; he needed the love that comes from the redemptive, life-giving nature of God. Sidamo needed grace and new love, and so did we.

The first thing we did was write out promise cards with two Scriptures on each one, and we placed these under all the mattresses he slept on. This way, he could rest on the promises of God. We believed the name he came with, Sidamo, was part of a grief that God was redeeming him from, so we prayed for a new name. With God's leading, we gave him the name *Samuel* for this season in his life. In the Bible, Samuel was such a child of promise and destiny. We had to speak this same kind of promise and destiny over this broken little boy and believe for God's vision for his life.

We carried him around each day, all day, snuggling him close to our bodies while worshiping and praising God over him and speaking God's Word over every area of his life. Since Destiny was nursing our youngest biological daughter, Galilee, at the time, she even tried to give Samuel the same. We did not have the medical equipment to keep him alive, but God is much bigger than that. For the first four months, each day seemed to get more and more difficult. Almost every week we had to seek God for new wisdom and revelation as to how to care for baby Samuel. Each day we had to dig deeper and rise higher for a new kind of love—one that was far beyond our human nature to give—and for a love that would give life to someone battling to survive.

Our flesh showed itself too often, and as much as Samuel needed grace to survive what was inflicted upon him, we needed grace to survive our own flesh. Each day we had to receive from God that which we did not already have.

God gave us a number of breakthroughs. He gave us words of wisdom from praying friends and family, revelation from His Spirit, and strength to give more love and grace to Samuel. God brought us an incredible nanny to help during the days and another believer to help pray and praise over his life. Eventually, this nanny became a very special part of our leadership team in Ethiopia. And she too had her love challenged through this fearfully and wonderfully made little boy.

We received Samuel when he was about 6 weeks old, after being born approximately two months premature. We noticed early on that, along with the tormenting panic attacks, Samuel could not make eye contact. He lived in what we can only describe as a fog that seemed to consume him.

One night, I had just finished feeding him and was heading back to bed while praying for him when the Lord suddenly gave me a vision. It was a simple picture, but a dreaded one. It came amidst my prayers for Samuel and seemed to be in regard to him as well. The picture was of a person cloaked in dreary, lifeless oppression. It was not a picture of death, but it was the epitome of the lack of life. There was nothing horrific about the look of the person in the picture, but the impression the Lord gave me of the vision made me think of the thief and stealing life.

I happened to Skype with my mom the next morning. I began to tell her of the vision, and she was amazed. That same day, before I called, she had just been reading something further on deliverance regarding cases beginning with similar trauma as Samuel had in the infant stage. She knew God was confirming something because the vision I described was so similar to some of the testimonies she had just read.

That day, our whole family fasted for Samuel and inquired of the Lord to gain insight of how to pray. God gave us about eight promises or bullet points to specifically pray, declare over him, and trust God for His deliverance and freedom. Aynalem and Mercy sat on the floor with Destiny and me as we gathered around this precious but hurting boy. We laid hands on Samuel and had a very simple prayer time, taking the authority of Christ and simply declaring the verses and words God had given us over him. Immediately, we saw something break open. And within 20 minutes, Samuel began to make eye contact with us for the first time. The fog that once plagued him began to dissipate, and we soon noticed that the frequency of his tormenting panic attacks began to slow down incredibly.

Two days later, Selam, Samuel's nanny, came over to the house for her time with him. We did not tell her anything of what God had done. But within 30 minutes of being with Samuel, she came running into the room, "What happened to him? He is so much different. What happened?" We laughed together with joy and thankfulness, simply sharing that God had set him free.

We had a few more instances such as these where God brought us tremendous breakthrough or a word of wisdom, where we saw healing or were led into a new strategy of love. And we needed every one of them. Our love never felt like enough, and that was the truth. We needed more, not just for Samuel, but for every other person we would come into contact with for the rest of our lives.

This precious little boy, Samuel, was a fighter. He had no medical care for six months while dealing with these conditions as a premature infant. He lived off of the lifeline of God's grace. We all did.

We later found out how much Samuel was up against while in our care. Our cousins from the States were prompted by God to adopt Samuel and saw God expedite the process in unbelievable ways. They traveled to Ethiopia, and Samuel was officially taken into their family. Even when he arrived in the U.S. with his new family, six months after we received him, the doctor who checked him immediately declared his condition as "failure to thrive." Before leaving us, he still could not eat, and what he did eat usually all came up. He vomited on average about 30 times per day. He was immediately diagnosed with cerebral palsy, and tests actually showed that his brain was literally split in a very unusual way. He has since had a number of surgeries on his stomach to help him keep food down. He was given a feeding tube and was even placed on valium at all times so that he could bear what his insides were going through. Finally, on top of everything else, the doctors found out that Samuel was legally blind.

Samuel is a part of our lives we would never change. For us, the circumstances of his life and the task put before us were like that 10,000-pound boulder God asks someone to push. Many times, we felt like absolute failures and the worst of sinners to not be able to make it move. Now we know that God never intended for us to move this particular boulder. Jesus simply wanted to ask us the same question He asked Peter, so that we would be prepared as Peter was prepared: "Do you love Me?" I think of Samuel, and I hear that question. I think of Samuel, and I can't even begin to share how difficult a season that was. I think of Samuel, and I think of someone who changed our lives *far* more than we changed his.

MICAH

Micah is Samuel's new name. It is part of the redemptive grace God poured out on Samuel when *He* moved that boulder. God moved the mountain in Samuel's life and brought Micah into a new, lavishly loving family that was the *perfect* fit for his life of promise. The parents who adopted him are our cousins. They have fought and battled, and praise God, they have seen incredible advances. His sight is returning. His ability to function is constantly rising. He is growing by leaps and bounds, his eating is progressing, and he is exceedingly loved! Micah has been an answer in their lives just as they have been such an answer in his. It is a beautiful picture of the Spirit of adoption and how God is moving among His children and in His family.

> *For you did not receive the spirit of bondage again to fear, but you received the Spirit of adoption by whom we cry out, "Abba, Father"* (Romans 8:15).

Sidamo and Samuel both shook and cried out pain in terrifying panic attacks. But Micah has been drawn into God's family, where now he cries out, "Abba, Father" according to the redemption and love God has used to give him life and life more abundantly.

THE NEW LOVE

This is the love Jesus challenged Peter with. This is the love Jesus challenged us with. It is a love that goes to a new level, beyond human understanding. It is an *agape* love. *Agape* love is described as "undefeatable benevolence, unconquerable goodwill."[1] *Our* affectionate or compassionate love is not enough for the calling God has for our lives to give life to those like Micah. We must have a love that is "undefeatable" and "unconquerable." This is the very love God has bestowed upon us. And like with Peter, who was a "fisher of men" who caught few, or none, until Jesus challenged His love over and again and strengthened the net in his life, Jesus wants to lead us to the other side of the boat. The other side is where God's redemptive and abundant catch resides and waits for us to arrive. The path to that side is a new love. Jesus is not questioning the affection of our love; He is challenging our love to become supernatural, undefeatable, and unconquerable. He is challenging us to walk in a love so powerful that we can begin to live life, and give life, on the other side of the boat.

ENDNOTE

1. James Strong, *Strong's Exhaustive Concordance of the Bible*, Greek #26.

Chapter 9

ACTS 4 GENERATION

…Freely you have received, freely give (Matthew 10:8).

THIS is how we are called to do life. Freely receive it, and freely give it. This is the most natural theme of how the disciples lived in the Book of Acts, according to what Jesus first modeled during the Gospels. If we are going to become life-givers, we too must have this mandate from the Lord engrained within our very beings. No matter the subject of the giving or the receiving, the nature of doing all that they did so freely marks the generation that came forward in Acts. The same open-armed, open-handed freedom must mark this generation as givers of life!

The disciples were in position to give life to the huge extent to which God used them because they put themselves in position to receive life more abundantly. Receiving life more abundantly here in Acts 4 is what empowered the disciples to walk into their calling as those who freely gave life more abundantly to their generation and the generations to come. Both these abilities are equally essential to the power that comes from the kind of generation that rose up in the Book of Acts: They were ones who knew how to *receive from* God, and they knew how to *give* freely *with* God.

All my life I was blessed to have a very unconditional, open-family kind of love modeled all around me. I had a family that prayed, a family that lived by faith, a family that reached outside themselves, gave freely, and saw God's full circle redemption fulfilled in people's lives. It was an incredible model to grow up with on a number of levels. And it is one of the reasons why Acts chapter 4 has always been a favorite of mine. There are several other factors that move me in that chapter as well, but the example my family portrayed and passed down to me as a heritage has had more effect than I could ever know. My current family and I began to run with this testimony while living in Ethiopia, at times not even realizing we were picking up this testimony and living it out.

But even if you have not had a family that has modeled this or a family that has passed down this heritage, you still have such a testimony available to you, waiting for you to grab hold. If you do, it will lead you into such a reformed, life-giving culture that you will begin to model this same kind of Acts 4 pattern to your generation, and you will hold it to pass on to the next.

Acts chapter 4 is not where the New Covenant believers first received the Holy Spirit, but it is a place where the disciples walked in *more* of Him. They found themselves united in one voice to the Lord, believing God with one heart and one soul for one purpose, which only He could empower them to live out. The disciples came together as a group of apostles—transformers of culture—and were empowered to live beyond the fears and doubts they battled all throughout the Gospels. They were empowered to live lives of freedom and of excessive, impossible fruit.

As these transformers of culture came together in Acts 4, they were launched far beyond human intentions, they were sent out with more than words or plans, and they gave beyond self in such a way that no one in the community had any lack.

This brought the beginning of a great harvest, and it began when these disciples *lived out* the extreme nature of their Teacher, Jesus. No longer did they only abide by His teachings, but they abided in the Teacher's very nature. Jesus' teachings took such root in them that transformation occurred and caused life more abundantly to ooze and overflow from their lives in a generation-reforming kind of way. They lived as apostles when they became "doers" and not "hearers only" (see James 1:23). They made the principles of Jesus' life and teaching such an uncompromising part of their own community that it changed their whole generation. They didn't start a new ministry or organization. They simply began walking like Jesus had taught them to walk. What is even more, they did so together in the power of unity. Freely they received, and now, freely they gave. Just as my family has left a similar testimony to me, Jesus and His followers have left this testimony for all of us to pick up and carry to our generation and the ones to come.

> *"Now, Lord, look on their threats, and grant to Your servants that will all boldness they may speak Your word, by stretching out Your hand to heal, and that signs and wonders may be done through the name of Your holy Servant Jesus."*
>
> *And when they had prayed, the place where they were assembled together was shaken; and they were all filled with the Holy Spirit, and they spoke the word of God with boldness.*
>
> *Now the multitude of those who believed were of one heart and one soul; neither did anyone say that any of the things he possessed was his own, but they had all things in common. And with great power the apostles*

gave witness to the resurrection of the Lord Jesus. And great grace was upon them all. Nor was there anyone among them who lacked; for all who were possessors of lands or houses sold them, and brought the proceeds of the things that were sold, and laid them at the apostles' feet; and they distributed to each as anyone had need (Acts 4:29-35).

They had unity and power. They had a hunger and desperation. They had a freedom from their old ways. The Holy Spirit was the One leading and empowering them, and they gave as quickly, if not more quickly, than they received. They allowed their lives to become a constant overflow between God and the world. When I look at this chapter, I see His Kingdom come. I see a group of believers who finally *lived* as apostles because they so partook of their promised land that they could share it with everyone here on earth.

Our calling as Christians is to be like Christ. Oftentimes, we learn from Christ much like the disciples did in the Gospels. But our calling is not just to learn from Christ; it is to *be like* Him. *"He who says he abides in Him ought himself also to walk just as He walked"* (1 John 2:6). The disciples realized they weren't supposed to simply be disciples anymore. Now they were to each live out His teachings in a radical sort of way.

The generation that came forward in Acts came forward because they knew there was something more. They lived it! Like the believers in Acts, we must not be content to be followers alone. Jesus allowed His followers to do so for only three years. I never want to stop following Him, but at some point I have to make a choice for more and desire to live *like* Him.

A time of transition, a time of more, was upon them. Now it was they who would help the blind see, the lame walk, the lepers be cleansed, the deaf hear, the dead be raised. Now they would preach the

Gospel to the poor, feed the 5,000, and live out a life of extraordinary love and power. When are we going to transition in this same way? We must receive life before we can give it, but we can only receive so much before we must start giving it away.

Jesus' command to the disciples in Matthew 10:6-8 looks to me exactly like what they began living out in the Book of Acts.

> But go rather to the lost sheep of the house of Israel. And as you go, preach, saying, "The kingdom of heaven is at hand." Heal the sick, cleanse the lepers, raise the dead, cast out demons. Freely you have received, freely give.

In Acts 4 we hear of this generation of culture transformers who gave life freely, in both spiritual and physical terms. They took their lids off and poured out without fear of having enough left over for their own lives. They took their lids off because doing so wasn't only a way to give, but it was how God would continue to refill them. Like the old saying goes, "You can't out-give God." They knew that their mandate to freely give did not come without the promise that freely was also the way they would receive.

We cannot be an Acts 4 generation of life-givers until we remove our measuring lines. We measure what we have, what we don't have, or the results in and from our lives from earthly terms. As long as we do this, we will be held captive from this reforming, life-giving lifestyle. We must not be such a measuring people, but a people of freedom in all that we give and receive. If we, like the apostles, will cry out with *one* voice, look at God's family around the world with *one* purpose, and put our trust in *one* Source to fill us, send us, lead us, defend us, and fuel us, we too will be part of an uncommon community that sees life multiply farther than it ever has before. We will be a generation that walks in power, overflows life, and knows no lack.

THEY ASKED FOR MORE

"Freely you have received." We have to remember this statement when we begin to come to the Lord for anything. Whatever we need within His will and purposes is free! This allows and even teaches us to ask for more. We must ask for more.

Freely the disciples called out for more of what they needed to fulfill their calling:

> *...They raised their voice to God with one accord... "Now, Lord...grant to Your servants that with all boldness they may speak Your word, by stretching out Your hand to heal, and that signs and wonders may be done through the name of Your holy Servant Jesus"* (Acts 4:24,29-30).

God was the only One who had more. They knew it was free, and so they asked for it. We have not because we ask not. *"Ask, and it will be given to you; seek, and you will find; knock, and it will be opened to you"* (Matt. 7:7).

As I mentioned at the beginning of this chapter, I have been blessed by the heritage I have inherited from my family. There is one testimony in particular that has given life to many in and through my family. In fact, I feel like I receive life every time I hear it repeated.

My mom grew up with three siblings, and her family was rather poor. Her dad had been very ill with a heart condition and was in and out of the hospital at least half of every year. Through this health crisis, they reached a time when their businesses all went bankrupt, and they could not pay their bills. They were renting a house and had little food available, and my grandma was working six days a week just to survive. She was exhausted, and her husband was in the last year or so of his life. The crisis only seemed to increase when the owner of the house they were renting approached and told them they had to be out immediately, as he was converting the property into a bank.

As mentioned, my grandma was exhausted. She did not have enough time, energy, or resources to do all that was necessary for her family. Her husband was slowly dying, and she surely didn't have enough money for another house.

One day—her only day off that week—she began to drive the neighborhood with my mom, who was about 9 at the time, and her younger sister, then 2. As soon as my grandma began to even look for a house, she was already exhausted. The overwhelming need and task she was called to walk through felt like too much. But my grandma had never been much of a feeler; she was a believer. They had just begun their search when Grandma pulled off to the side of the road and declared, "Let's pray!" "Lord," she cried out, "You know we do not have the money for a house, and I do not have the time to look for one. But You know we need a house. So Lord, we ask that You would give us a house."

As simple as that, they turned around and went on with the laundry list of needs to survive. The next day, a neighbor from across the street came and knocked on their door. "I am being transferred," he said. "You need a house, and I don't need this one anymore." He lived across the street in an enormous house that spanned three lots. "I would like to give you my house. You don't need to give me a thing, as I understand your current situation. Maybe sometime in the future we can work something very small out for payment, but I do not want you to worry about it."

My grandma, my grandpa, my mom, my aunts, and uncle were desperate, but they knew that they served a God of "more." Even their prayers did not have to be extravagant because they knew a God who was and is extravagant in His grace and giving toward us. The next day, the whole family and their friends literally formed an assembly line across the street. From the house they had to vacate to the one they had just been given freely, they passed item after item: from family member, to friend, to family member, to friend across the street, and through the door until the house was full. They asked for more, but they *received* more than they could even ask for.

We need to be people who live *in* more because there is *more* already within us. We spend much of our lives pursuing more of the wrong things; we need to learn to channel that same vigorous hunger to the right kind of "more." My family was desperate when they cried out to God for more. We can learn something from this, but not just for those times when we are desperate. What if we applied the miracles we hear and speak about from desperate situations to our lives and calling *before* we became desperate? Sure, these desperate situations will still find us now and then, and we can seek God in the same way then, just as my family did. But what if we became *proactive* with our desperation? What if we sought the more that is available to us before the need arises? Instead of only asking for more when we need it, let us live desperate for more so we can give more to everyone all the time! We give life to the world, circumstances, and people around us by giving them more of God. But first, we must learn to ask, both when we are desperate and even before we are desperate.

THEY RECEIVED MORE

My grandma and her family were losing their house, as well as her husband, my mother's father. They trusted in a God of "more," and *more* is what they got. They were given an even larger house right across the street. And more than the provision itself, they were given new life in their faith, which only fueled their ability to give more life to others. They lost the life of my grandfather about a year later, someone I never knew, but they saw God begin to give new life into the family, the extended family, and many friends and acquaintances through receiving that house. Freely they received the life that house brought to them, and then for years after, freely they watched God use their family and that house to give and multiply more life than it ever received.

When we ask God for more, we always receive even more than we bargained for. It's free! That's what His grace means. It's available. And when He pours out the life that comes with more, it is always meant to multiply. When we learn to receive from God, what comes in can always go out bigger, deeper, wider, and fuller than when it was received. That is God's nature as the Life Giver: He is fruitful, and He always multiplies. He is not the question. Our ability to receive such grace is the question that must be answered. Only then can we *give* life with Him.

The apostles in Acts 4 experienced the exact same kind of receiving. Freely they received more than they could ask for because they asked for the right kind of more.

They cried out with prayer in this way; then they began to receive as freely as they asked. They received one of the most powerful answers in Scripture because they received something that began a multiplication that could not be stopped.

> *And when they had prayed, the place where they were assembled together was shaken; and they were all filled with the Holy Spirit, and they spoke the word of God with boldness* (Acts 4:31).

Their current surroundings were "shaken." Something rocked their world. God answered them and gave to them in such a way that when they received what He had to give, even the place they were staying was not left the same. Something beyond human answers came into that room. Why is it that we expect so little of God? What would happen if we asked and received like the apostles in Acts 4? God always wants to exceed our meager expectations. We must learn to ask according to the more He is capable of and according to the more of *who* He is.

When the apostles asked, they did so because they knew they needed more of Life Himself to fulfill their calling. So they put themselves in position to be filled up. They took the position of expectant prayer so that the answer God would give could give life to them and to many more.

Destiny, our firstborn daughter, Mercy, and I took a trip five years ago that changed our lives forever. It started with us asking for more, and it continued and finished with us being carried by grace through more of an answer than we were ready to receive.

I was working with Youth for Christ International at the time to coordinate their global youth prayer movement. As we looked at that role, mixed with the calling and mission God had been putting before us for years, we sensed God's calling to base somewhere other than the United States. We knew we were called to give life to the broken and empower the powerless so that they could give life to others. But before any of this could happen, we needed to receive an answer from God that would empower us to give. He was calling us to step into a new position to receive.

CROSSING THE JORDAN: RECEIVING MORE!

The trip was going to cover seven African nations in seven weeks. We would fly into Rwanda in February and leave for home from South Africa in April. We had five other nations in between, with trainings we were scheduled to facilitate and a lot of people to meet and learn from. The trip was a way of asking God where He wanted us to be based and how He wanted us to give life. But first, little did we know, God would use this trip to give new life to us so it could multiply to others.

Even though the trip was scheduled, we had very little of the funding for the flights or expenses involved. But even a couple weeks out from our departure date, we still felt a strong peace from the Lord that we were to go, regardless of what our funding or circumstances looked like. I asked the Lord about our need and simply heard, "It's done, go! Just as the Jordan was not parted until the Israelites stepped into the water, you must step and you will walk through the river on dry ground." So that's what we did. We could not fulfill our calling to give life without God giving us new life through a miraculous path—on the other side of the Jordan. We had to cross over. We had to walk in more before we could give more.

We had enough funds to purchase our ticket to Rwanda in February, and we purchased our return from South Africa in April. But we had no flights firmly booked in between them. We were told by all our contacts in the various nations of what we needed for food, lodging, transportation, and so forth, and it totaled about $3,000 just for those daily expenses. We only had $500 for a family of three and all seven nations. But God!

Our travel agent tried to hold onto spaces on as many of the flights he had set up as possible, so they would be available for us when provision came through. However, the spaces would be taken up quickly. In the meantime, we boarded our first flight and were on our way to Rwanda.

Our time in Rwanda was one of the longest of all the nations we visited, and according to their words, they "exploited" us. Wow, did we feel it! But it was well worth it. We met so many amazing people, formed incredible relationships, and saw God bring forth lots of fruit. But our trip came to its end, and we still did not have funding for our next flight to Ethiopia. The day before we were scheduled to leave Rwanda, we checked into how much the flight to Ethiopia would cost if we purchased it at a local office. It was $1,400 for the three of us. We continued in prayer and kept walking forward toward God's purpose.

By late that afternoon, we received word that $1,400 exactly had just come into our account, and it was wired immediately from the office in the States to us in Rwanda. Praise God! We even ended up on the same flight we would have left on had we been able to take the original flight our travel agent had scheduled. Not only did we receive provision for the flight, we received more faith.

While on the flight to Ethiopia, I began to inquire of the Lord how we were to get to our third stop, Kenya, at the end of our time in Ethiopia. Apparently I had received more faith than I had previously, but still wasn't full enough yet, as I was already worried about the next flight! But God's grace and faithfulness are bigger than me, and the Holy Spirit began to give me strategy. I felt led to seek out our primary contact in Ethiopia upon arrival and ask if she knew of a Christian travel agent. So, on our way from the airport to the hotel late that night, I asked. Amazingly, she had a good friend who was a believer and a travel agent and assured us she would take us to see him later in the week. Before leaving Rwanda, we had checked with the airline what it would cost to go from Ethiopia to Kenya, so that we would be prepared. We were told all three tickets would cost $1,100.

The time in Ethiopia was going very well, and we immediately sensed a connection in our spirit—one that started even as our plane touched the ground. During our first few days in Ethiopia, no new provision had come in toward our trip. But the morning we were scheduled to meet with the Christian travel agent, we found out that $600 had just been deposited into our personal account. It was just over half of what we were told the tickets would cost, but we were thankful to receive any provision at that point. We arrived at the travel agency, they brought us some incredible espresso macchiatos, and they began to check our flights. When the agent asked for our passports to book the tickets, I had to ask how much this was going to cost. "Six hundred dollars," he answered very casually. We handed him our personal debit card attached to the account where the $600 had just been deposited that morning, and suddenly we had our tickets to our next stop in Kenya.

As we mentioned before, we had only $500 cash to cover all our food, lodging, and expenses. In Rwanda, costs were at a minimum because we were blessed to stay with a local missionary family who helped us immeasurably. In Ethiopia, we incurred about $300 worth of expenses, leaving us with $200 for the next five nations.

Knowing this, our contact in Ethiopia told us the one thing we would want to do was avoid staying at one particular guest house in Kenya, which would cost us $500 alone for the length of our stay. So, upon arriving in Kenya, one of our first questions was to ask where we would be staying. We laughed—and maybe cringed a little on the inside—when they told us we were staying at the exact same place we were just warned not to stay. But our Kenyan contact told us it was the best place for us to be and that we would have one month to pay our bill, which gave us a timeframe extending through the first week of April. Praise God, He gave us a safe, nice place to stay and provided through the grace of time.

Our time in Kenya involved more travel than hands-on ministry, as we viewed different aspects of the local ministry and the country. But the final day, the day before we were to travel to a new nation in the south of Africa, Botswana, we were supposed to lead training with their volunteer team of young leaders.

Most of the trainings we led were patterned off of Acts 4, teaching the individuals how to come together, inquire of the Lord, seek God's vision and strategy, and be filled up and prepared for Him to send them into His purposes for their lives and ministries. This required some teaching time, but it also included a lot of practical prayer and waiting on the Lord as we taught the participants how to go into God's presence to be empowered by Him. Destiny and I were overwhelmed during this time watching how moved by the Spirit this team was.

They were one of the most united groups we met with, and thus, when they came together to wait on the Lord in prayer, they experienced even more than others had. Unity always increases our ability to receive the life and the "more" we are asking God for.

We were moved during the prayer time, but we were overwhelmed and humbled as it concluded. Just as we were wrapping up an incredible time in God's presence, the local director, who knew of some of the miracles God was pouring out during our travels, rose to her feet and began sharing some of the testimony of God's provision on our trip with the group of volunteers.

Before she could even finish her last words, one young volunteer stood up and walked to the kitchen to grab a bowl. The young volunteer had something to say to the whole group; "We are not leaving here until this family has enough money for their flight tomorrow to Botswana." (The need by the way was $1600.) Our eyes got even bigger, our jaws dropped, and tears were pouring down our faces. In fact, I can hardly think back on this time without weeping. Humbling does not even begin to describe it. This young leader lowered the bowl near his pockets and just started emptying. He passed the bowl around and everyone did the same. These were volunteers at a local Youth for Christ mission in Kenya. They had no salary, very little for themselves already, and now they took everything and began to pour it out on us. What an example of being open-handed and giving freely regardless of circumstance. We were broken and so ministered to over this outpouring of selfless, abundant love.

The leader then took the bowl of money into a nearby office belonging to a national ministry they were connected to and began to tell those people the testimony of how God had just moved. Before we knew it, they were so moved by the extravagant, free giving of the young volunteers that the office decided they would believe God for the difference until it was provided. The next day we got on our flight to Botswana overwhelmed by how God, once again, had poured out not just what we needed, but He had also allowed us to receive much more from the nature and testimony of His love.

Once we arrived in Botswana, we knew that we had to buy the rest of our flights in one chunk, including stops in Mauritius, a small island out east in the Indian Ocean; Madagascar; and finally South Africa. This chunk would cost us $4,000 from start to finish for the flights alone—of which we had nothing. But we knew God had not allowed us to miss any of our schedule, and we had not even been late for one meeting despite relying only on God to take us across the African continent one miracle at a time.

We had less access to communication where we were in Botswana, and I was very sick. Our account showed no funding available. But we had to keep moving forward by faith so that we could receive what God promised to give, a grace only He could give. God had to supply if we were going to walk into a season of our lives where we could give life in the way God had called us to.

Two days before we were to leave Botswana for the island region of Africa, we got an email that the exact amount needed for our tickets—the full $4,000—had just come into our account. We were elated and just praised God! This chunk would get us through each of our last stops and back to South Africa in time for our mid-April return home. We called our office in the States to contact our travel agent immediately. However, we were met by some sobering news. All the spaces he had been holding for that $4,000 total were now gone, and we were back to square one. The only flights available now required an extra flight to make one of our connections, and the total was almost $6,000. An amazing co-worker who was Stateside and helping us in our communication back home said she would look around some more. We said we would continue to pray and believe, and I told her we would look forward to hearing good news soon.

We went directly to our knees and thanked God for all He had done already. We had been walking through this river on dry ground, and we had not even missed or been late for a meeting while crossing the continent. In fact, we reminded the Lord of this, claiming His faithfulness and promise that we would walk through the river on dry ground. We held it all back up into His hands and left it there before we went to sleep.

I woke up to the phone ringing the next morning. It was a phone call from our office in the U.S. "Joey, it's a miracle! You'll never believe what happened! We got the space. Now you arrive early, and we even added an extra connection that will eliminate the bus ride from Botswana to South Africa. And now the tickets will cost less than four thousand dollars."

We rejoiced together before heading into the rest of the day. Once again, God had given us more so that we would have the opportunity to go and multiply and give that "more" away.

After Botswana, we had a very busy but wonderful trip in tropical Mauritius. Someone referred to it as the Hawaii of the Indian Ocean, and wow, were they right! It was a fantastic week going into God's presence and seeing the youth empowered by God in new ways. If that wasn't enough, the island itself was breathtaking. Being there was one of those "abundant" blessings in the trip where God lavished even *more* on top of the promise we were already receiving. We stayed in someone's home right on the beach in Mauritius. They welcomed us into their family with open arms and blessed us beyond measure. We left for our flight to Madagascar that first week of April. We had become very aware of the date the night before we left because our guesthouse bill in Kenya for $500 was now due.

We were still living off of the initial $500 expense money we had started with. Having our money make it this far was already like water turning to wine, but we did not have enough to pay the bill. We woke up that morning before our flight and kept looking up, knowing the Lord still had more to pour out. As we went out the door, we found an envelope on the table from the family we were staying with. Inside the envelope was exactly $500. This was starting to get crazy! But we serve a crazy-abundant, life-giving God who has crazy amounts of love to pour out on us. We just have to step into position to freely receive the same grace He has called us to give freely to others. God put us in that position to teach us to receive the life He wants us to give.

After this miracle, we had an amazing time with the team in Madagascar. What a wonderful place—and what incredible people. We had several days of awesome sessions and growing relationships with people we still love and miss today. God did a few other miracles during this time in the islands. Then we landed for just a couple days in South Africa to wrap up our trip, meet with some leaders, and board a plane back home.

However, just before we left for the airport, I could not help but grab a piece of this life-giving testimony we had just received from the Lord. It would be a key in our calling to give life for years to come. God gave us far more than a vision trip across Africa. He gave all three of us more life—not just provision—than we ever bargained for. So, as we walked out to the van, I scooped up three rocks: one for Destiny, one for our daughter Mercy, and one for myself. Those rocks were proof of the testimony, for us and for others, that God had indeed led us across the river on dry ground. That trip changed our lives. Those miracles hadn't been in our plans, but God wanted to give us more. He was simply asking us to cross over by faith.

The Israelites could not walk into the abundance of their promised land without receiving new life before crossing over. That new life and fresh, renewed faith empowered them to step into the Jordan, to see it parted, and to cross over into the "more" God had waiting. We have to receive new life before we can walk into new life. Only then will we be aligned with the Life Giver to give new and more abundant life to the world around us.

When we receive from God, it should not be an isolated instance that leaves things unchanged. The answers God wants us to receive should go beyond our human capabilities and overflow in a way that only His grace can sustain us. We can only give what we have received, and we can only receive what we are prepared to give. Like the catch of 153 fish in John 21, we should be surprised we were even able to receive as much as God wants to pour out. This means that we learn to lean on His grace to take us somewhere we cannot function without Him. That's what the disciples asked for in Acts 4. They knew their weakness and were OK with that. They just called on God, asked, and then received *more!*

> And when they had prayed, the place where they were assembled together was shaken; and they were all filled with the Holy Spirit, and they spoke the word of God with boldness (Acts 4:31).

The grace God poured on the apostles in that room was world-changing. It was full of a new power that could only come from God. The disciples did not go out in their own intentions or great ministry ideas; they went out empowered and sent by the Spirit of God. God filled them up with a grace that would give life in ways they could not give on their own. The level we receive freely from God is the level we can give freely and powerfully with God. We must position ourselves to receive what only God can give. He is the Life Giver; being a Giver is foundational to *who He is.*

THEY GAVE MORE

Because of the life God had poured into the apostles when the room was shaken in Acts 4, they had faith to give more than what their generation was accustomed to, without measure. They had all things in common, they shared all things, and no one called any of their possessions their own, yet no one had any lack. Freely they had just received in Acts 4:31; now, in verses 32-35, freely they gave:

> *Now the multitude of those who believed were of one heart and one soul; neither did anyone say that any of the things he possessed was his own, but they had all things in common. And with great power the apostles gave witness to the resurrection of the Lord Jesus. And great grace was upon them all. Nor was there anyone among them who lacked; for all who were possessors of lands or houses sold them, and brought the proceeds of the things that were sold, and laid them at the apostles' feet; and they distributed to each as anyone had need* (Acts 4:32-35).

I wrote previously of the miracle my mom's family experienced with their house. And I began to hint at the "more" that God had given them, beyond the physical structure of the house. When they received that house from God, they didn't hold onto it for themselves and protect the one thing they could lose again. Instead, they began to freely give away what they had freely received.

I can't even begin to count how many people besides their immediate family unit lived in that house over the years. They stayed for one season of life or another—days, weeks, months, even years at a time. Rooms were filled with people who had similar level needs as my grandma and her family had faced the day they received that house from God. My family could have gone on defense and protected this precious gift that was all they had. Instead, despite their supposed lack, they gave all the more freely. Countless people who had been robbed by the thief in one area of life or another were given life so that each person who stayed there could find life more abundantly.

A funny thing happened: God's Kingdom principles came to life. The more they gave freely, the more they continued to receive. This life-giving cycle became stronger and stronger over the years as God kept giving them more than they could give away.

A few years ago, at my grandma's funeral, the most difficult thing after losing her presence in our lives may have been limiting the number of people who wanted to say something at her memorial. See, that free house she received sowed incredible amounts of life into countless people because she gave it away freely each and every day. Person after person wanted to stand up and share the life they had been given—new life, new hope, and opportunity—because of even a brief stay in Grandma's "family" house.

My grandma and her family had nothing at the time, hardly enough to survive on themselves, yet they still took what they had in their hands and found a way to give life each and every day to more and more people. This life continued to multiply through each of those individuals and their families as well. Oftentimes we excuse ourselves from God's life-giving example because of what we do not have. But God is not asking us what we don't have; He is asking us to open our hands and our hearts with all that we do have.

This life-giving testimony from Grandma has been passed down to multiple generations. My mom and my aunts and uncles have all carried on that same heritage with their houses and families. There has been an open door and open hand policy in all their lives, as they never held on to what they might have, but *always* let it freely flow back out for the sake of giving life to another.

Family holidays in my hometown are wild now. You never know who will be at the family gathering or what new or broken soul might have joined the family. At Christmas we have to remember to call the host to find out who may be coming whom we don't know about so we can make sure and have something to bless them with. My grandma's free house from God became a family life-giving foundation that has given life to so many spiritual sons and daughters. It was never a formal ministry, nor did it need to be. As this practice continues in our family members' homes now, it still is nothing more than giving life to those who have had it stolen from them by freely giving all that we have freely received.

My grandma's house was an Acts 4 house. Those who stayed there were welcomed with love and brought into God's presence through prayer. Everyone shared, and no one left with any lack.

This is a lot like the house God told David He wanted to make him. As we mentioned in Chapter 2, Giving Life, David wanted to build God a house, but God had a better idea. He would turn David into a house—a family that had a legacy of descendants. It was a house formed out of sons and daughters who had received life and who would give life and multiply. The multiplication continued through Christ Himself. Many times, we feel a calling has to come through a formal ministry. But more than any building, God finds His house within His family. Oftentimes while we are developing programs to minister, we are missing the opportunities right under our noses to give life to someone in need, someone else who has been created to multiply. You don't need a ministry; you just have to freely give what you have in your hands, as you might give to your very own family.

It did not matter what ministry we did in Ethiopia; nothing was more powerful than the house of multiplication God began through family. All our current leadership team came from building family: the life-giving relationships within our home. Some of these people lived with us. We threw weddings for others. Some worked in our home when in need of a job, and others came over to meet and go into God's presence to be filled up and sent.

We went to Ethiopia to build a house that could empower God's children into His purposes. When we left, God had given us a house that looked a lot like my grandma's—bearing both a physical and spiritual resemblance. We met people in need, and they came in and took what they needed. We did not have extra funds for ministry, but we had what God had given us in our home, and everything He gave us we saw multiply through people. It never grew while in our hands or possession. But it always multiplied and gave even more life once it had been given away.

As a life-giver, we have a choice in life. We can live according to measurements or toward multiplication. The smallest seeds contain the most abundant life, yet so many of those seeds stay locked up in our possession. We have buried for fear of losing them or have counted them as nothing because we do not see through faith to what is inside. In Acts chapter 4, the apostles did not just go out to minister. They came in to meet with and be filled up by Life Himself. He filled them so full that they began to overflow the power of God, physically and spiritually. Because it was His Spirit who filled them, they ministered in power much more than by effort or intention. They were so full that they gave freely, and still no one knew any lack. Simply put, they were open—open to receive the best parts of God and still able to overflow all that God poured in.

Can you imagine what would happen in this world if we as the Body of Christ became an Acts 4 generation of life-givers? If we tapped into the deepest parts of Life Himself to live and give according to a power that is beyond us? We must get so full of Him that we freely give love and life to everyone around us, not through the measures of ministry, but through loving them and giving our lives to them as if they were family. That is, after all, the same kind of family love our Father has given us. God did not send Jesus to build a ministry; God sent His one and only Son to give life to His family. Jesus came to us as if we were family, to freely give His life so that we could receive life more abundantly. What are we still here for if not to live and give like Jesus, like Boaz and Abraham, and to give away that same life each day?

The Church in Acts 4 was a generation of life-givers who learned mission through a new perspective of walking in new power. They gave life freely and ferociously because they looked at the world like family, and their mission was fueled by the One who fueled them. Freely they received life, and freely they gave life. *The multiplication was unstoppable!* God is calling us to live life and do mission with a new perspective and new power.

What, or Whom, do you have in your life to give, and who is passing through your day who needs it most? We can be an Acts 4 generation. We simply must take off our lids, receive directly from God, and freely overflow to the world. We will be in the world, but we're certainly not of it. Give life! Be fruitful and multiply.

Chapter 10

VISION OF TRANSFORMATION: LION-LIKE

EVERYTHING the Lord had begun in the vision of that fruitful and abundant promised land was coming alive and changing my perspective. It was altering the way I both saw and gave life. I saw that so much more was available, right at our fingertips. The taste of Heaven was available to share with all those in need. The Lord had said I could take of what was His and declare it to the world!

I—now—want to live *that* way! I never want to forget the power and abundant life that is freely available not only to me, but through me! I now realize that truly, it's already in me. I never want to give someone anything less. I realized I have more to give now than I ever had partaken of or shared before.

I dropped to my knees to seek the Lord and His change in my life. I needed to surrender more of self, more of my lid that kept Heaven out of me and prevented Heaven's promises from being revealed through me to the world. So many of my thoughts and mindsets needed to go.

My selfish and limited versions of God and His Kingdom had to be let go, shattered, renounced, and traded in for something more. I needed more of Him. I fell to my face and sought the Lord.

A verse found its way to my heart:

> When one turns to the Lord, the veil is taken away. Now the Lord is the Spirit; and where the Spirit of the Lord is, there is liberty. But we all, with unveiled face, beholding as in a mirror the glory of the Lord, are being transformed into the same image from glory to glory, just as by the Spirit of the Lord (2 Corinthians 3:16-18).

My heart longed for Him! I needed a change; I needed more. I needed to lose the veil of self I had seen Him through all these years. The veil had been removed on His side for sure, but what about mine? Had I kept up a veil?

Still seeking the Lord, eyes closed, I turned my head to the right and found Him. The impression of His fatherly face appeared like a cloud, or like a silhouette, but with all the same fatherly love radiating upon me. I felt so unworthy. But His love picked me right up from such thoughts and feelings.

I blinked for but a second and looked again, but now in the same place was the image of a Lion's face. It was the Lord, the Lion of Judah! He opened His mouth as if to speak, like a gentle roar. He said nothing, but a translucent smoke consumed me as it came from His mouth. He had breathed on me. The Lion of Judah breathed His breath over me, like a consuming breath of protection and love, and I was taken in.

Next, He opened His mouth as if to speak again. This time His roaring breath was not like smoke, but like fire. What I thought would burn me instead left me untouched. The Lord was firing off old stubble from my selfish life, like burning the chaff out of wheat. My half perspectives of Him, my insecurities, my fears, and my doubts were swept away so I could *see* life, *live* life, even *give* life in His abundant form. The fire was the purest thing imaginable. Once it touched me, I welcomed it. His breath was a loving and consuming fire, consuming even the smallest chaff of self so that nothing counterfeit could grow in the purity of His Kingdom life and promises.

I looked down momentarily to take in what had just happened. And when I looked up, I saw a mirror in His face. I could see the reflection of self. Still, I needed more. His mirror revealed that, if anything, I needed to be transformed from any part of self so I could walk fully in His Kingdom promises, receiving them freely and giving them with wide open hands to those who hungered for more themselves.

After circling through my thoughts, I looked up at the mirror of His face again. Now, I was changed. The mirror still bore my reflection, but now my reflection was that of a lion. I was a lion! I looked like Him! What greater joy than to bear His image! I was beside myself. It was the most wonderful thing I could imagine because my reflection had been transformed from me to Him, the Lion of Judah.

I heard a voice, but He wasn't around. It was not the voice of one speaking out loud, but rather that still small voice rising up from within. "Be strong, and very courageous!" The words were like a balloon rising in the sky, but instead they were in my heart. "Stand in courage to live beyond yourself, to give beyond yourself." Still, the words were but a wind in my soul. But I knew inside what He was saying. I could not live this life-giving life if I did not stand courageous against the world and all its pressures. I could not live this life-giving life if I did not step courageously in ways that were against the world's pull. I could not give life if I was not courageous enough to give what He had helped me receive. I had to give the best parts of my promised land. I had to have courage enough to live in this world, but pass out His. That would take courage. I had to have courage to love the lost and broken like family, the courage to love and give outside the lines. I had to courageously go on offense, paint with never-before-seen colors, and call out life, purpose, and destiny. I had to courageously stand up in the boat amidst the storm and speak His peace and authority over the storm's push. I had to live the courage of a lion—not just any lion though, the Lion of Judah. Jesus stood in such courage, even in the face of the cross. I saw His reflection in me now. I had felt His consuming fire, and I was in transition from one who bore the glories of self to one who lived the glory of giving life. I had to have courage to ignore and live beyond self. I needed the courage to live beyond self-consciousness so I could live in His promises. He was not only bringing me into this land of promise; He had given it to me!

THE GIFT

I looked over where the Lord had first met me, and He was back. This time He simply handed me a gift. I could tell the gift had a sense of strategic timing and meaning. It was a red box with brilliant white ribbons. I was struck by the red box and even wondered, *Why the red color?* I opened it, sensing great anticipation from the Lord. It was important to Him.

I opened the box and there was a wristwatch. It had red leather bands and striking gold fixtures. Again, I was struck by the red color. It seemed so purposeful. I asked Him, and again, instead of hearing the answer out loud, I heard His answer rise up from within. The red resembled His blood, His grace. The gold was the very definition of His royalty—and ours as sons and daughters. I inquired of Him further and began to understand the power behind the gift.

He gave me the gift so that I would know the grace of His timing. I had to know the grace He had given me for this season, for each day, *the grace for this time to live and love as unique, life-giving sons and daughters of the King!* His grace is my ability to receive freely, and I had to know what and how to receive freely from Him if I was to give life freely *with* Him. His timing was different from my timing, and He had a grace He wanted me to walk in for this season of my life. He had a grace that would be my life for this season, and therefore, it would be the grace I would give life through during this season. This watch was a gift representing my need to know the grace He had set forth for this season in my life, which would correspond with the season His will was releasing on earth as a whole.

If I did not embrace the grace of God's timing, I would try and walk in His season according to my own ways and perception—and would likely do so with the same mindsets I had before. But I had to align with Him. I had to align with the grace He had called me to walk in, the new things He is doing, and I had to align with the timing He had set forth for that grace to be released. I know God has different seasons and timing for all of us; He uses different ways for each of us at different times in our lives. I had to know His grace for right now, and for each day or season that was to come. There was a hidden seed of life in me that only a son or daughter could have, and now was the time to multiply that life to others in a fresh, new and life-giving way. No longer could I be lost within the timing or perspective of self, for He had a greater, more strategic timing and focus.

I had to know the purpose of this season of life so that I could receive freely from Him and give freely with Him. This is the time for His grace to come to life in me in its fullest form. It is time for me stand up, stand out, and freely overflow the special grace and unique life He has given me. I was beginning to understand the grace He had given me to walk in for today. I could not try to walk in any more or any less, but to be who He created me to be—for this time. I could not look at others, measure, or compare. In fact, others would be waiting for what He has put within me. God had graced me with different gifts long ago, just as He has each of His children. Those gifts of grace would now come out specifically and powerfully during His seasons and His timing. As a son, I carry a special DNA of life that could not be hidden or kept in any longer—it had to multiply, and it was ready to do so now! I had to join His purposes, and this watch would help me do so much more efficiently. "Thank You, Lord!" I cried out.

WORLDS AND PROMISES COLLIDE

I started to seek the Lord again, pursuing His nearness, to worship. I looked up toward the heavens where I would often picture Him on His throne as I approached in worship. However, I could not connect. The Lord was not within my expectations or ways. But I had to find Him. I longed to worship Him. I continued to seek Him and continued to search for Him, tirelessly. I knew He was near and wanting to be found. He was growing me, shattering my ways and expectations, so I could grow further into His. I kept trying to rise up to worship Him, but I still could not connect as my heart so wanted.

And that's when He came. He wasn't on a heavenly throne; He was right before me. I had not risen up, but by His grace, He had come down and met me on my level. He never asked the woman at the well to rise up to His level, but instead He met her uncompromisingly where she was. He was giving me the same grace. I wanted to rise up, but He wanted me to receive the grace of Him coming down. Grace—and my ability or inability to receive—was center stage in my heart.

As soon as I received Him in the way He was meeting me, rather than where I was looking for Him, I saw that we were immediately back in that heavenly, fruitful promised land He had lifted me into before. Only now, it did not seem that I had been lifted up at all, whereas before I felt divided, like my feet were on earth, but my heart and head were in the heavens. There was no divide at this time; instead, it became apparent that there was what I could only describe as a "great collide." Wow! Everything was different. Two worlds collided and meshed into one. I could find neither the ceiling of earth, nor the floor of Heaven. By grace, Heaven was meeting earth once again.

The Lord directed my attention to my right, where Adam was again walking up to us. Only this time, Adam was naked. I have to admit, I was a little uncomfortable, but neither he nor the Lord seemed uncomfortable at all.

"Even beyond disobedience," Adam began to speak to me, "my greatest loss in the garden was my ability to be freely naked. To be naked is to have no veil, no self-consciousness or insecurity in your perspective, no loss of vision. Before I ate of the fruit of the tree of knowledge of good and evil, I lived freely and was all the better for it. God's heart didn't just ache at my disobedience; He ached because He knew what I had just subjected myself to: self. I had divided my vision and focus and had taken away my own ability to freely receive because now I had to hide my nakedness and could not freely receive or give all God had available to me. God did not take anything away; I did. I took away my own freedom. I made myself self-conscious."

"The grace of God allows us to be freely naked, without veil, so that nothing—no part of self or human perspective—can separate us from Him and the hope of His calling. When I lost this grace, my mind and focus were forever divided between living out my calling and protecting my own pride. To be renewed from your efforts to refine self you must become freely naked and unveiled again, allowing only His grace to cover you. Only then will you freely receive all that is available to you, that which is necessary to give life."

The Lord stepped forward and began to speak. "You cannot give life freely from My promises unless you also receive freely. You have a saying, 'It is better to give than to receive.' However, I must remind you that if you do not know the grace of receiving freely from Me, without worry of the nakedness this grace exposes, then you will not have what it is you are called to freely give."

"It is the battle over grace. You work for, earn, and are faithful for none of this promised fruit; it is free by grace through faith. Where My Spirit is, there is freedom. Freedom comes from grace, and it is free. This land, and all of My promises, are free. You do not have to come up to get them and distribute; you simply must learn to receive and walk in My grace in a new and more complete way."

"My grace is sufficient for you, and My strength is made perfect in your weakness. This does not mean you are to use My grace to refine your weakness; rather, My grace completes your weakness. This is what you must freely receive. Your weakness is not always to be despised or worked on, just surrendered. Rejoice in your weakness, and you will find My strength. Rejoice in your weakness, and you will find My fruit and My life. It all comes by grace through faith. You must have more faith in My grace to meet you where you are than in your effort to rise up to Me."

"There is no shame in receiving grace, and it is not a one-time gift. Instead, it is a continuous, promised flow of the abundant life of Heaven. So many receive My grace and then walk forward on their own. But if you want Heaven manifested and pouring out on earth, then freely you will continue to receive grace, and freely you will give the very same."

"Grace is My abundant life. It is the life that multiplies, and it must become the world you live in. Grace does not set you up for a Kingdom calling; rather, grace is your Kingdom calling. You must not just be weak in order to become strong; you must continually rejoice in your weakness so I can pour out My best gifts at all times."

"If you will see my Kingdom come and this fruitful land of promise come to life in the lives of those who need it so desperately, you must be OK with being weak on earth. You must be OK with being misunderstood or persecuted for My sake. You must be OK with not having the answers and even with failure itself. In the world's view, failure is dreaded, but those in Heaven see it as an opening for My promises to finally pour out. What looks like failure on earth is often strategic in Heaven. The law measures failure, but grace gives life! The more you are OK with remaining poor in spirit while on earth, the more My Kingdom will be available to you and through you. When you have learned to freely receive, and only then, you can freely give of the promises I have shown you."

"Grace, My child, is yours. If you will give life and life more abundantly with Me, you will approve your weakness, receive My abundance each day, and live a life of freedom, freely receiving the fact that you live off the free gift of grace. I came to give life and life more abundantly, because I came as Grace. Let grace come to you as often as possible. For as often as you freely receive grace, you will become one who freely gives life."

I finally understood. The Lord was not calling me to rise or to measure up; He wanted to come down. He did not need me to be refined; He needed me to be open. Our human nature makes us strive to rise, perform, and cover up our weaknesses. But His loving, grace-giving nature can only pour out when and where there is an opening to receive. The lid I put on to protect myself from weakness takes away His strength of pouring out His grace. I had to put myself in position each day to receive grace so that I could give life. A promise I remembered from Jeremiah 45:5 struck me deeply as I recalled it: *"'...I will bring adversity on all flesh,' says the Lord. 'But I will give your life to you as a prize in all places, wherever you go.'"*

Most of us want to earn or prove something as we gain or even give life, but God wants to give our lives to us as a prize in all places, wherever we go. The sooner we start receiving our lives freely from the Lord, the sooner we can freely give God's best heavenly prizes away to those who need them most. Then, they can begin to multiply as well. Grace was the seed I needed to receive and give each day. Then I would be a life-giver in the worldwide family of my Father.

"Thank You, Lord, for Your grace." I cried out. "It is my life." My Life Giver had given me a seed, and now, by His Spirit within me, it was ready to multiply!

THE VISION COMES TO LIFE!

It is time for us—the children of God—to arise! It is time for us to walk in the grace God has put within us, a grace that is more lion-like than we might know. There is a special grace, a unique piece of God's image inside each of us that is waiting to give life to the world. It's a grace that we often keep locked up for fear of how we may look or appear to others. But now is the time for us to live in courage, the courage to be who God has created us to be—the courage to maximize His grace in our lives and let it freely overflow to the world. We must have courage to live like sons and daughters who have life *more abundantly* already inside of us! It is time for us to go beyond telling the world about our Father's Kingdom and have the courage to *show* them!

It takes courage to walk in the fullness of grace, to allow ourselves to be weak while knowing His grace *will* be strong—stronger than anything this world has ever seen. It takes courage to live by faith and walk out our front door each day freely living as the lion He sees inside us. It takes courage to believe in the supernatural power of grace inside us, waiting to flip the life that is all around us into something more *abundant*. It is time for courage! It is time to rise up as sons and daughters—children of the King who are lion-like—who have a different and more abundant kind of grace inside us than much of the world has yet to taste. Don't be afraid to live like a lion, like our Father. There is a Kingdom life inside us that the rest of His lost sons and daughters desperately need. He has given us a special grace for this time—have courage!

Conclusion

THE LIFE GIVER
IN YOU

THERE is a new vision before us. The same vision that was lost in the Garden of Eden has been given back—a vision of new life! God has given that new life to anyone who believes—what we do with it is up to us. The life He has given us is more abundant than we first realize, and it is already within us. There is abundant life inside us that cannot be measured out or controlled, but which must be freely released to overflow to our worldwide family in need. As we freely receive and freely give, He *will* take care of the rest!

We have long sought, like David, to build God a house. However, God is giving us the same answer He spoke to David, *"I will make you a house."* He is making us a house, not a physical structure, but a family structure, built of sons and daughters, fathers and mothers, those who will take the life He has revealed within them and let it multiply freely!

As we connect to the Life Giver and see the world through His lens, He will release an offensive move of multiplication through us that will change the world. Life more abundantly comes to life in us and through us when we move from defense to offense. It comes to life when we move from being actors, who are subject to life, to directors, who give life to everyone in the scene and story. The Holy Spirit is waiting to reveal this kind of life to the world, the deep unseen things of God's Kingdom, which He makes freely available to all who will believe. But will we turn our palette to receive His colors and paint freely in His most creative and life-giving ways? Love never fails, and it always brings life! Love is, in fact, the most supernatural thing on earth—overcoming death—and *always* breeding life!

There is life inside you, and it is more abundant than you may know. You know it as grace, a small seed that the world has heard about for years. But inside that simple, familiar seed is a life more abundant than much of the world has ever known. In that simple, familiar seed is a land of promise that is waiting and wanting to come alive in you and give life to the world. Life more abundantly is already within you, but it is up to you to live out the courage to *believe!*

ABOUT THE AUTHOR

JOEY LeTOURNEAU lives with his wife, Destiny, and their four daughters, Anna, Aynalem, Mercy, and Galilee near Denver, Colorado, after three years living in Addis Ababa, Ethiopia. Joey and Destiny travel extensively, empowering God's children to draw near to their First Love, and live out the testimony of Jesus to the world around them.

You may contact Joey at:

Joey.letourneau@gmail.com
www.mark1014family.com

In the right hands, This Book will Change Lives!

Most of the people who need this message will not be looking for this book. To change their lives, you need to put a copy of this book in their hands.

> *But others (seeds) fell into good ground, and brought forth fruit, some a hundred-fold, some sixty-fold, some thirty-fold* (Matthew 13:8).

Our ministry is constantly seeking methods to find the good ground, the people who need this anointed message to change their lives. Will you help us reach these people?

> *Remember this—a farmer who plants only a few seeds will get a small crop. But the one who plants generously will get a generous crop* (2 Corinthians 9:6).

EXTEND THIS MINISTRY BY SOWING
3 BOOKS, 5 BOOKS, 10 BOOKS, OR MORE TODAY,
AND BECOME A LIFE CHANGER!

Thank you,

Don Nori Sr., Founder
Destiny Image
Since 1982